ATTRACT YOUR IDEAL MATE BY
BECOMING AN IDEAL MATE

LATEZES
BRIDGES

Single Wives by Latezes Bridges
Published by Success & Beyond Global Enterprises, LLC, Atlanta, Georgia
PO BOX 1753, Douglasville, GA 30133

This book or parts thereof may not be reproduced in any form, stored in a retieval system, or transmitted in any form by any means — electronic, mechanical, photocopy, recording, or otherwise — without prior written permission of the author, except as provided by United States of America copyright law.

Unless otherwise noted, all Scripture quotations are form King James Version.

Scripture quotations marked NIV are from the Holy Bible, New International Version. Copyright ©1973, 1978, International Bible Society. Used by permission. 1984

Scripture quotations marked ESV are from the Holy Bible, English Standard Version. Copyright © 2001 by Crossway Bibles, a division of Good News Publishers. Used by permission.

Scripture quotations marked NLT are from the Holy Bible, New Living Translation, copyright © 1996, 2004, 2007. Used by permission of Tyndale House Publishers, Inc., Wheaton, IL 60189. All rights reserved.

Book cover and interior design by Ursula Nokonoko
Edited by David Good

Copyright © 2015 by Latezes Bridges

All rights reserved

ASIN #: BOOBSJQTGQ
E-Book ISBN-10: 0615778968
Printed ISBN-13: 978-0615778969

Second Edition

Printed in U.S.A.

THE PURPOSE OF HUMANKIND

GENESIS 1:26-31

26 Then God said, "Let us make human beings in our image, to be like us- god-like. They will reign over the fish in the sea, the birds in the sky, the livestock, all the wild animals on the earth, and the small animals that scurry along the ground."

27 So God created human beings in his own image. In the image of God he created them; male and female he created them.

28 Then GOD BLESSED THEM and said, "BE FRUITFUL AND MULTIPLY. FILL THE EARTH and GOVERN IT. REIGN OVER the fish in the sea, the birds in the sky, and all the animals that scurry along the ground.

29 And God said, "See, I have given you every herb that yields seed which is on the face of all the earth, and every tree whose fruit yields seed; to you it shall be for food.

30 Also, to every beast of the earth, to every bird of the air, and to everything that creeps on the earth, in which there is life, I have given every green herb for food"; and it was so.

31 Then God looked over all he had made, and he saw that it was very good! And evening passed and morning came, marking the sixth day.

FOUNDATIONAL PRINCIPLE OF LIFE & RELATIONSHIPS

Before we are able to effectively function in any relationship, we must first know and understand our:

1. IDENTITY
2. PLACE OF ORIGIN, ANCESTORY, or LINEAGE
3. PURPOSE & DESTINY
4. POWER
5. POSITION OF OFFICE & AUTHORITY

In life, it is essential to operate in and on purpose. If we do not know the purpose of a person or thing, the inevitable result is abuse (improper use) of the person or thing. Therefore, it is necessary to learn the purpose of humankind-people-husbands and wives before entering into relationships & marriages as to prevent abuse.

Humankind (Individuals): We are blessed. We are purposefully designed to prosper, dominate, rule, and govern our environment.

TABLE OF CONTENTS

Acknowledgements	15
Special Dedications	17
Preface	18
Introduction	21

Chapter 1
Self Discovery — 37

Single Wives Defined	38
Learn From My Personal Experiences	42
Life Experience is the Best Teacher	46
My Journey to Wholeness	52
A House Divided Will not Stand	54
God Help Me; How Do I Find My Husband	59
Purpose: Are You Working On Your Assignment?	65

Chapter 2
Journey to Wholeness — 68

Setting Healthy Boundaries	73
Never Settle for Less than You Deserve	78
Identifying Hidden Road Blocks to Attracting True Love	85

Chapter 2, cont'd

Fear Blocks Faith Action	86
Identifying What Love Is Not- Love Is Not Abuse	92
The Effects of Lies, Rejection, & Betrayal in Past Relationships	105
Letting Go of The Past Moving Forward	113

Chapter 3
Dating God's Way — 114

Decide What You Want in a Man	114
Dysfunctional Relationships Examined	119
The Devastation of Divorce	127
Healthy Relationships Begin With Healthy Friendships	135
Godly Husband Checklist	143
Self-evaluation: Are You desperate to date?	154
Single Wives Dating Boundaries	159

Chapter 4
God's Plan for Marriage — 166

Why Do Marriages Fail So Often?	169
God's Original Design: Marriage 101	177
Marriage Roles and Assignments	184
The "S" Word: What Does "Submission" Really Mean?	190
Sexual Fulfillment: Preparing To Meet His Needs	202
Practicing Love; True Love- God's Love	204
Are You A Wife?	208

CHAPTER 5
Manifesting Your Mate:
Mind Mouth Manifestation (MMM)   **220**

Mind-Mouth-Manifestation: Fighting Fear With Faith   221
What Do You REALLY want?   224
The Single Wives Basic Priority Plan: Preparation is Key   226
Manifesting Your Mate: Speak Those Things   228
Single Wives Affirmations   232

CHAPTER 6
Single Wives Manifesto   **236**

About the Book   244

ACKNOWLEDGEMENTS

Special thanks to my parents, Douglas & Patricia Judkins and Samuel & Celeste Bridges for providing me with love, Godly counsel, parental wisdom, and support all of my life. You guys consistently motivate me to excel beyond business limitations, remind me that you are proud of me, and encourage me to keep fighting the good fight of faith! I'm always strengthened after our time together. Love my parents! Family is everything, and I'm thankful for each of you. To my special cousin Amanda Sunshine Williams, thanks for all of your encouragement, you rock!

An extra special thanks to my mom, Patricia Judkins, who has been a constant visual of God's love demonstrated towards her children and others. Thank you for teaching me how to love everyone, help those in need, and to be an intelligent and virtuous woman. You are a priceless jewel. May all of your dreams and heart's desires manifest expediently!

To my siblings and dear family: Patrick (Antonio Nino Love), Latoria, Julie, Monique, Yasmine, Jasmine, Kelvin, and Sheneya—I love you guys so much! Family is everything, and I'm thankful for each of you.

To my friends Kera Lewis, Kenya Young, Kanika Turrentine, and Hassan and Fransmise Kingberry-thanks for the special support and personal motivation that you all have given to me through difficult life transitions. Thanks for encouraging me to birth this book in your own way. Pastor Charles Price (Papa), you have been a continued source of encouragement and wise counsel in this season of my life. Thanks for supporting me in ministry and teaching me to stir up all of my gifts from across the globe. Blessings to you and your ministry!

To all those who have provided me with internal inspiration, external motivation, and the real life experiences that fuel my writing. Thank you, I really couldn't have done it without you!

May the divine insight and revelation that you will read within these pages bless, heal, and deliver you, and ultimately propel your life from one season into the next, in the mighty name of Jesus! Amen.

SPECIAL DEDICATIONS

This book is dedicated to all women who are seeking God for direction, guidance, and instruction as you prepare for your marriage mate.

To my beloved big brother Douglas Judkins Jr., (Spanky) words cannot begin to express how life has been without you. You brought so much joy and laughter to our lives. You are greatly missed. This book is dedicated to your memory. I love you.

PREFACE

So many women are stressed, depressed, and super-anxious about "getting married" when they don't seem to have a true desire, accurate biblical understanding, or the basic relationship skills necessary to help them stay married. Contemporary social norms and the media diminish the importance of the institution of marriage and distorts marriage's proper function. Our society is more accepting of divorce than in times past, and the media is sending messages through films and reality shows that divorce is the way to go if your marriage isn't working. However, who really wants to wait a lifetime to get married only to have a relationship that doesn't work and ends up in divorce?

Society, in general, seems to misguide us about marriage—the purpose, functions, and the expectations for each person within the marriage. Most Christians agree that marriage is an ordained institution supported by God, but they don't necessarily agree on why. Most people of faith could not answer, definitively, if asked why marriage is important to the body of Christ and society, at large.

Maybe this ambiguity surrounding the purpose and importance of marriage is a contributing factor in why the divorce rate is over 50 percent within the Christian community. In turn, this extremely high divorce rate could signify society's lack of understanding about how marriage should function and our general inability to make it work according to its purpose.

God designed marriage to be a mutually beneficial and permanent institution. We need to revisit the designer's manual, the

Bible, to obtain a more accurate understanding of what marriage is and how it should function. When the marriage model is properly operated and not abused, this will allow the users to experience the true benefits of marriage.

We invest so much time, energy, and money into our education and profession, yet we do not invest much time preparing for the lifetime commitment of marriage. Taking the proper amount of time to prepare for marriage would be wise, as this is an institution that you plan to be in for the rest of your life.

Much of my varied education and life experiences have led me to explore the various issues related to why singles are struggling in relationships and why marriages seem to be failing more and more each year. I am a trained sociologist who has extensively studied human behavior, family dynamics, social deviance, and psychology. As a bi-lingual (Spanish-English) family intervention specialist, I've been solicited by international businesses, the U.S. Department of Education, colleges and universities, the Federal Court System and countless churches and youth and family serving agencies to develop culturally-tailored training curriculums or 12-step programs that would assist families from all walks of life and backgrounds to overcome relational challenges.

As a licensed minister, evangelist, and spiritual coach, I've counseled hundreds of women of all ages, with diverse experiences and relationship statuses. All of these women have sought guidance, emotional healing, and deliverance because they felt resistant to positive change, unable to progress in life, and unsuccessful in relationships. They claim to have been unable to prevent themselves from dating or marrying men who were not marriage material; these men were ungodly, immature, financially unstable, verbally or physically abusive, unfaithful and unfit fathers. As I began to work with these women in the areas of inner healing and deliverance, it became evident that they were suffering from the multi-faceted effects of childhood traumas and unresolved pain due to various dysfunctional relationships that prevented them from developing a healthy relationship with God and others. They lacked proper instruction and guidance from spiritual leaders in the area of overcoming the various natural and spiritual challenges of living a successful christian life as a single woman.

My prayer is that this book will be a valuable resource to Christian singles and that they would receive the healing, deliverance, and Biblical understanding necessary to prepare them for success in relationships, in general, and marriage. This book provides important knowledge necessary to obtain and sustain a healthy relationship, the prerequisite to successful marriage.

Enjoy.

INTRODUCTION

You are going to LOVE the information in SINGLE WIVES. This book will prove to be a life-changing guide to catapult you from singlehood to a successful marriage.

"Proper prior preparation prevents poor performance" in whatever you set out to be successful at in life. Why would this not be true for marriage? Oftentimes, we tend to prepare for various endeavors in life that are far less weighty than marriage and leave our marriage's success to chance. What a fatal mistake!

THE CHURCH'S CRY FOR HELP

I'm a regular guest minister on the TCT Television Network, and I'm astounded at the staggering number of family support requests that come from church-going Christians who are completely unhappy, unfulfilled, and who have no clue how to resolve major issues within their marriages. Statistics show that more than 50 percent of marriages fail inside the Christian community and roughly 60 percent of second marriages fail, and once you have gotten to a third marriage the outlook does not look good at all. What we are left with is a society full of broken, wounded children and adults who have witnessed the breakdown of their families. Therefore, they have distorted views on how families should function because of the dysfunction that they have witnessed. Without help, these same people tend to have difficulties attracting and operating in healthy relationships.

Without seeking the proper guidance to recover from past traumas, they end up going into new relationships with tons of "emotional debt" or baggage. Have you heard the expression "hurt people hurt people?"

Well, this is exactly what happens when people attempt to engage in healthy relationships but have not healed from the internal wounds left from previous traumas. The church pews are full of hurting people who feel imprisoned and bound by negative emotions and painful experiences and just can't seem to break free to live the abundant life, which includes hsuccessful relationships.

BASIC EFFECTS OF CHILDHOOD TRAUMA

Many of these individuals have experienced childhood divorces, parental neglect, domestic abuse, molestation, or witnessed a loved one who was addicted to drugs or alcohol. They do not know how to effectively cope with the feelings associated with these past traumas, so they just bury the emotions of their experiences deep inside.

Do you know that whatever negative emotion or unresolved pain that you bury within yourself will manifest in other forms within your life? Unresolved negative emotions will manifest in the form of physical or emotional illnesses, psychological or mental challenges, or self-destructive behaviors like drug or alcohol addictions or engaging in unhealthy relationships.

BREAKING FREE FROM BONDAGE

Thankfully, seeking professional counseling has become more widely accepted among underrepresented groups and the church when personal or family challenges arise. Consequently, during the past few years there have been a large number of men and women in the church who are more openly expressing their constant struggle to break free from emotional bondage. They all are being terrorized mentally with daily reoccurring negative thoughts of past or current disappointments, defeats, fear, anxiety and depression. These negative thoughts come as a result of experiencing past hurts, abuses, betrayals, rejections and ultimately relationship failures. These negative episodes have left long-lasting stains on their hearts and in their souls that now affect all other relationships in their lives including their relationship with themselves and God.

THE CYCLE CONTINUES UNLESS BROKEN
I've spoken at countless churches and community events for singles desiring to please God in their singleness while awaiting their marriage mate's arrival. I've learned that there are a few main reoccurring challenges in everyone's situation. More than 90% of the married couples and divorced singles that I've taught, coached or ministered to were not ready to get married when they did because at that time of their nuptials, they did not understand what marriage was all about from a proper perspective.

I've noticed that many individuals that I have encountered had gone from one failed relationship to another without taking any time to evaluate their previous failures or to heal from the effects of emotional damages inflicted during those past relationships. As a result, there were no "lessons learned," no personal growth, or emotional development experienced, thus making them a prime candidate for another failed relationship in the future. There must be specific time set aside to evaluate your life—especially after experiencing a failed relationship to get an understanding of what happened, why it happened, and how the situation has affected you.

Obtaining this basic information about all of your previous relationships will tend to show you a pattern or cycle of behavior in your life. Knowing your dating or relationship pattern will be the first step in helping you to identify any consistent poor decisions or missed lessons that need to be learned so that you may make wiser choices for yourself in the future.

DON'T GIVE UP ON MARRIAGE

I'm finding that more and more of my friends are beginning to grow exhausted with the entire "marriage thing" and are starting to feel that they should give up on the idea of experiencing a happy marriage. Divorce is so commonplace in the media that finding examples of healthy marriages with truly happy people isn't an easy task. Consequently, many people are adopting alternative ways to enjoy romantic companionship, sexual fulfillment, and child rearing.

No matter how attractive alternative marriages are presented in mainstream media, school systems, and even in some churches, it is not God's plan. It's a counterfeit that contradicts God's purpose for the family model and procreation of humankind.

Without getting back to God's original plan, that marriage should be between one woman and one man who would raise their children up in the admonition of Christ-demonstrating an example of tight-knit unity, there is little hope for the body of

Christ or mankind for that matter. God specifically instructed the first couple, Adam and Eve, to be fruitful and multiply. He mandated them to bear children physically (childrearing) and spiritually (mentoring) so that God's family would increase in number and strength to win more territory and souls for the Kingdom. What will happen if this multiplication doesn't occur? We should think about this, seriously, in terms of how we should connect with people and strategically form kingdom-based alliances, as godly marriages.

THE BIRTHING OF THE SINGLE WIVES BOOK

I'm an entrepreneur, a visionary and a business consultant at heart. I have an innate desire to assist people to find solutions to their problems. I call myself, "The Solution-ologist." If there isn't a likely solution, then I create one. I've always been moved or inspired to create businesses, programs, and product ideas with the ultimate goal of teaching people to break out from beyond the barriers in their lives so that they may achieve success and beyond in every area of their lives. These are two organizations God put in my heart to birth to help build His Kingdom through business and ministry.

Beyond the Barriers Outreach, is a family-centered and community-focused non-profit that provides educational programs and scholarships; crisis assistance and targeted supportive services for at-risk populations. We aim to teach each person to destroy every barrier; mentally, physically or emotionally, that prevents them from living a life of purpose. Similarly, Success & Beyond Global Enterprises is a multi-faceted consulting agency that provides bi-lingual (Spanish-English) business solutions for individuals and corporations.

What does Beyond the Barriers and Success & Beyond have to do with SINGLE WIVES?

In our business trainings and/or outreach support groups, we teach participants the importance of having the proper perspective as it relates to our beliefs about achieving a goal. If you believe that you are incapable of being a multi-millionaire with a happy and fulfilling life then you are not likely to pursue a path that would help you to achieve those goals.

I am a contributing relationship blogger for JENNINGS WIRE, THE WORLD OF SUCCESS, and I recently posted a blog titled "Stuck on Single." It basically listed some potential reasons why ladies who desire a compatible mate are not finding them.

The same mental processing required to achieve a business goal is used for achieving relational goals. You must believe that you are capable of having a happy and fulfilling relationship with your God-ordained mate so that you will work towards achieving that goal. If you truly believed that you could have the marriage of your dreams, then you would be making decisions that are in line with that belief. This may include not choosing to date men who are incapable of loving you as God intended, and abstaining from abusing or dishonoring your body with drugs, alcohol, or pre-marital sex.

If you truly believed that you will have the loving mate and fulfilling relationship that you desire in your heart, then you would literally prepare yourself for it. While preparing for the marriage of your dreams, you would not settle for being involved in relationships that are below that standard.

THE BIRTHING OF THE SINGLE WIVES SEMINARS AND WORKSHOPS

I've noticed in most one-to-one spiritual coaching sessions, family intervention sessions, and church conferences, that there seems to be a strong need for targeted biblical instruction and real life application in order to help singles prepare for marriage and for married couples to stay together. They both need help to overcome personal challenges, which prevent them from being successful in relationships. Although many churches attempt to reach out to the singles and minster to them by hosting singles events, simply having a bi-annual dinner outing or movie night for them will not develop and heal them from past relational failures nor prepare them for the plight of marriage-since most singles do desire to be married. They need targeted training on becoming healthy from the inside out, and on being successful singles who bring God glory with their lives and ultimately marry without divorcing. In addition, pulpit preaching alone is often not enough for couples experiencing great relational challenges. It is not enough for the spiritual leaders of the church to simply tell married couples to "trust God, read your Bible, and just stay married" when people are dealing with highly complex relational dysfunction that stemmed from childhood trauma and when additional supportive services by trained counselors are necessary.

Many people have had failed relationships and need healing and deliverance in their emotions. Others have experienced divorce and need special support to grow forward. Everyone has been hurt in some way and needs to increase their self-esteem, understand how to choose compatible mates, and date appropriately with the goal of marrying to stay married. Most people want to do better and if they really could, then they would, but they need more training to do so.

PERSONAL EXPERIENCE IS THE GREAT TEACHER

I grew up with pastoral parents who taught me Christian values, and showed me love and support. Yet, I missed the mark by ignoring those values and entering into an ungodly marriage that ended in divorce. To grow from that relational failure, I had to seriously evaluate my life and address the decisions that I had made for myself, asking myself how and why did the divorce occur? Why did I choose to marry when that decision was contrary to what I knew in my heart was the best for my life? In processing my mistakes and choosing to grow from them, I had to overcome many misguided thoughts and beliefs about relationships that I had learned through my personal experiences with men and had adopted from poor role models. Because of my dysfunctional belief system regarding relationships, I had various misconceptions about how men and women should treat each other in romantic relationships. I had to ask myself many questions: What were healthy boundaries in courtships? What constituted as unacceptable behavior or abuse from a partner? What were true biblical role expectations for husbands and wives? What does "submission" really mean in a relationship or marriage? What are the appropriate ways to express love, first to myself and then to others? As a result of my misunderstanding of the aforementioned, I had many relationship "issues" that prevented me from attracting healthy relationships. My age was not important. I was immature relationally and needed mental and emotional development to grow as a woman who is prepared for marriage.

Once I learned and accepted my mistakes for what they were, I began to see the beauty of them. They were simply life lessons that would assist me in becoming more successful in this area in the future. I saw the success in my failures and grew forward. I was eager to share this newly discovered insight and wisdom with others with hopes of preventing them from experiencing unnecessary hurt and pain from making poor decisions. This book and subsequent seminars were birthed as seeds to address the supportive needs of singles, with the goal of teaching women how to build healthy relationships and families, and how to obtain and sustain fulfilling marriages which ultimately prevents divorce.

GOD'S PERSPECTIVE ON SUCCESSFUL LIVING AND RELATIONSHIPS

I feel that God desires for His daughters to live the abundant life; to travel and experience the wonders of this world and without struggling to make it in life. 3 John 1:2 (NIV) says, "Dear friend, I pray that you may enjoy good health and that it may go well with you, even as your soul is doing well." This tells us that our health, happiness, and good-fortune are, actually, high on God's priority list for His children. He wants us to enjoy life, be free of pain (physical, mental and emotional) and to be prosperous in all areas of our lives from the inside out. There is nothing glorious about struggling in your finances, health, or relationships all of the time—contrary to what some believe, it's not Christ-like to struggle and not have the things that you need to live happily.

There is a huge misconception that christians should not be wealthy, have the best of the best in life and enjoy a superior quality of life. I mean, that is how the royals live no? Absolutely! Well, we are royalty. Revelations 5:10 tells us that, "God has made us Kings and Priests and we shall reign in the earth."

We were given the power and authority to reign and rule over every challenge and demonic oppression, such as sickness (mental, physical or emotional), lack or poverty, and abuse. John 10:10 tells us that, "the thief came to steal, kill, and to destroy us, but God came so that we could have abundant life." I feel that living beneath God's standard of reigning, ruling, and living the abundant life is not His will for us.

In addition, I believe that lowly living, accepting poverty and lack (lack of money, joy, love, etc...) in any area of my life is demonic. It is my responsibility as royalty, a Queen, to take charge over those evil attacks assigned to derail me from living the abundant life that Christ died so that I might have. I believe God's Word, and I expect to receive all that it states is available to me. If God says that I can and should have something, then I want it and will not stop until I have it, all of it...every promise that He promised me!

The word "abundant" means that you have more than enough of everything that you need to live a happy life; there is overflow and surplus in your life. There is an excess of happiness, joy, pleasure, money and love! God is love so He would want you to experience as much of Him as possible, right? It is a misconception among Christians that poverty and oppression should be accepted as a normal way of life when the exact opposite is true. Once we accept our Royal status and Kingdom privileges, then we will feel better about living the best life possible and expect others to treat us as royalty with a high level of respect, as that is what we deserve. Lowering our standards for others should not be an option. We are Queens, therefore we should only date and marry Kings.

GOD GIVES SEED TO THE SOWER

I am anointed for wealth, and my life story is a testament to that. One huge factor that has contributed to my financial success is that I've always been a tither, a giver. No matter how much money I have at any given time, I consistently give to those who are in need. I give my time, my skills, my prayers and my money to help others as a way of life.

My parents demonstrated a life of self-sacrifice to others through giving and taught us that no matter what we are blessed to have in life, it is God who allowed it. God is the source of all the blessings that we enjoy and because of that we should remain humble and mindful of the needy around us. As such, I have made a lifestyle of giving. I give when I have little and when I have much, to various individuals, churches, and community projects that help needy youth and families overcome crisis and succeed.

I'm dedicated to living for Christ, and I work for Him daily. I've followed Matthew 6:33 which says, "if you seek first the Kingdom of God and His righteousness, then all other things (that you desire) will be added unto you." I make no more excuses for living and experiencing the Word, as this opportunity is available to everyone equally.

I'm not bragging. I'm saying all that to say that we, as God's daughters, must have a similar perspective regarding having prosperous relationships. We must put on blinders to all those who oppose you living the best life that you can. Make no excuses for it. You deserve the best of the best in your relationships because you are Royalty. You should set high standards for yourself and choose only mates that will treat you like a Queen by showing you love and the utmost respect.

This book is a seed, a testimony of God's faithfulness to keep his promises to His daughters, even through adversities and painful relationship transitions- such as singleness. These words are seeds of the Word of truth, deliverance, and divine wisdom to prepare God's people who are praying for loving relationships and healthy marriages to appear. This book is a faith seed for those who are anxiously awaiting the manifestation of their God-ordained mates. I'm sowing out of my season of singleness a labor of love to you, and this book will bring forth the manifestation in my life as well as yours in the name of Jesus!

PUTTING IT ALL IN PERSPECTIVE

You can gain the whole world and lose your soul, so I believe that true success comes when I do God's will and fulfill my purpose in Him. You cannot put a price on the success that you acquire by drawing others to Christ as you model a successful Christian life for others. This allows others to truly "see" and come to know Christ. Jesus' life was an example of successful singleness, as He was married to His ministry, living in full-time service to God. He spent his life helping the needy, facilitating healings and deliverances to the bound, teaching and disciplining others. He was completely connected to the source of all power and provision, God the father, which allowed him to operate supernaturally at all times. Jesus completed His God-ordained assignment until death and completely impacted the entire world for ages to come as a result of His obedience.

This is the model that I use to gauge my success as a single woman: How much am I changing the world For Christ? Fulfilling His purpose for my life? Being obedient to His will for me in every situation? I'm married to the ministry- Him, and He is my first priority.

Being married to God during singleness- making Him your first relational priority, having a deep connection to Him, and fulfilling His purpose for your life, will allow you practice in operating in your future marriage. This is the model for ultimate relational success- having the proper relationship with God, who is love, before we attempt to engage in relationships with others. You cannot give what you do not have and if you do not have God, then you do not have true love in your heart. This is a strange concept, but we must practice loving ourselves and others, with time we become better at it. God will help you to work out our love "issues" before we marry prematurely and potentially hurt our future mates. So take the time to perfect your love with God in your singleness as to assure that you "got the hang of it" before you marry and are able to give your future spouse the gift of true love.

PREPARATION IS THE KEY

Marriage is a wonderful institution, but many people wish to reap its benefits without sowing the hard work needed to build a healthy one. A solid foundation is built on the marriage partners having a solid friendship prior to getting married. True friendship is one of the main keys to successfully sustaining a mutually fulfilling marriage. The problem is many of us do not know what true friendship looks like because we have not had many people in our lives that would actually be considered true "friends" from a biblical standpoint.

I do not call every person that I have a relational encounter with a friend. Friends have specific characteristics that are not found in all people. Have you ever heard the saying that "good friends are hard to find?" Well, they definitely are. Friends are people who love and respect you for the person that you are while motivating you to excel and become your best self. Friends often desire more for you than you do for yourself; they wish to see you succeed in every area of your life and will not do anything to interfere with that process. They are supportive when you really need someone during a tough time, they are there to give you what you need so that you can make it to the next point in your life. Friends are assets to your life and push you in a positive direction towards your goals, purpose and destiny. Two great friends who join together in the divine partnership of marriage will both benefit from the union because they are both being supported and pushed towards their goals, purpose and destiny. Marriage provides endless benefits, but also requires extreme mutual commitment, investment and self-sacrifice to reap those benefits.

If you don't put anything in, you will not get anything out unless you are abusing your partner by allowing them to do all of the hard work that is necessary to make the relationship successful. You must practice the principle of preparation BEFORE YOU MARRY to ensure the intended result - which is a long-lasting union without ever experiencing even the thought of divorce.

WHAT DO MARRIED PEOPLE DO?

In this book, you will learn the original intent and design of marriage and the operational job descriptions of the husband and wife. This helps to assure that all persons intending to become married will have learned and practiced the operational role within the "marriage job descriptions" prior to the wedding. Prequalification is necessary for the role of a wife or husband, and if you really want the job, then you should prepare so that you will keep your job sustaining the marriage. It may seem odd to use the word job to describe the marriage role of a wife but the reality is that it is a full-time job that carries much eternal weight and earthly responsibility. If you are not ready to dedicate yourself to the job of being a wife as your first priority, then you probably should not marry. This book is not to deter you from wanting to get married by making you feel that marriage is "too hard." On the contrary, this book will provide an accurate representation of what it entails. It will facilitate a proper understanding of the expectations of partners so that you are not surprised about your duties when you get your job or become a wife. Yes, I said when you become a wife because my ultimate goal in this book is to develop highly qualified and prepared Single Wives. Single Wives are equipped to easily transition into roles of married wives who have experience in successfully sustaining healthy relationships thus decreasing the chances of divorce.

Basically, I wish to divorce-proof your marriage before you get married through providing strategic educational training and targeted preparation. You may not believe this, but marriage preparation starts way before you become engaged. It starts before the dating phase with an ideal mate- it actually starts before you even meet your potential mate! I submit that proper marriage preparation starts during a time that society calls "singleness." I actually call it the "marriage preparation" phase because in my opinion, a Godly woman is never really single.

Okay, all the women who have no significant other right now are saying, "What is she talking about? I'm definitely single because my lonely bed confirms that to me every night!" I do understand the feelings of loneliness, and I still maintain that you are not single if you a single wife. Let's find out why.

CHAPTER 1: SELF DISCOVERY

I'm sure that you are curious to find out exactly who are Single Wives. I'm excited about telling you! First, allow me to define a few important key terms. What is singleness? In addition to the standard definition of "single," which is often used in society to describe an unmarried person; it also is used to describe a "unique person" or "one who is set apart" for a specific purpose. I like to call it "top shelf" as you are high quality-suitable for a unique type of person.

So, instead of meaning that you are just "alone," "deficient," or "lacking something," my definition would denote that you are "singled out" and "set a part" for a specific timeframe to prepare for a unique purpose.

What about the term "wife?" A wife is defined as being "a woman joined in marriage to a man" or "a woman considered in relation to her husband." These are natural, standard definitions of the term, but we will explore the spiritual implications of the word more, later on within this book. I would like to draw your attention to a very familiar biblical text, Proverbs 18:22 that says, "He who finds a wife finds a good thing and obtains favor with the Lord."

Have you heard that before? Well the text specifically says that the man finds a "wife" and not a "woman" or a "female." Thus she is a wife before the wedding occurs, before he finds her! Other translations of Proverbs 18:22 says that the man who finds a wife finds a "great good," " a good treasure," or "a good life, and finding a wife shows that God is pleased with Him - that God has been good to him, and that he has obtained God's approval. What an incentive for each woman to make sure that she qualifies as a wife and a greater incentive for the men to hurry and find their wives to obtain a great treasure and God's approval!

SINGLE WIVES DEFINED

I mentioned that I would provide my spiritual definition of a wife and that role starts during our singleness. Single Wives, in part, are unique women, set apart for Godly purposes. They are healed from brokenness - whole women fully developed and prospering in all areas of their lives. They are, spiritually, physically, and emotionally healthy so that they may be a great good or treasure for their future partner who is a suitable mate for them. This does not mean that these women are exempt from challenges in life, but they bounce back from challenges by maintaining the proper perspective to continue growing and maturing according to Godly purposes. They have completed the internal processing of letting go of unrealistic expectations about love, relationships and marriage. They have healed from past emotional traumas that would have prevented them from experiencing true love. They have an intimate relationship with God, who is true love, and have learned to love themselves before attempting to love others.

Single wives make wise choices for themselves, in dating, by setting healthy boundaries in relationships and only dating men who are suitable mates. Meaning mates who are naturally and spiritually compatible, and meet the qualifications of Godly husbands - not just "boyfriends." They are confident and have high self-esteem because they fully understand their worth as Queens. They are extremely valuable assets to a potential marriage partner. They prepare themselves for the roles of "married wives" while they are single sives to ensure the success of their future marriages. Single wives are good treasures for their potential husbands and help them to have good lives and win favor or approval from God.

Women must undergo a developmental process to grow from simply being "women in waiting" to becoming single wives, so we must learn about that maturation process.

If you're reading this book, then it's obvious you plan to be married one day to a person who is equipped to give you the love that you deserve. You wish to stand in blissful matrimony with your spouse as a testimony to the world that God's plan for marriage actually works. If so, congratulations, you are well on your way to that "favored man" finding you and the two of you living your dreams of having a loving, happy, and fruitful marriage.

LOCATE YOURSELF

The first step in arriving at any destiny is to accurately locate where you are presently in relation to reaching your ending goal. You must be honest about who you are, where you are in life, and how you plan to accomplish the goal of qualifying for the role of a wife. You must be an ideal marriage mate to attract an ideal marriage mate which I will coin as "King Charming." If King Charming were to knock at your door looking for a wife, would you be an option? Would he select you just the way that you are right now as his suitable mate? The more direct question is, are you a woman "waiting to get married" or are you one of the SINGLE WIVES preparing to become a married wife?

SILLY WOMEN:
WOMEN IN DEVELOPMENT—SINGLE WIVES

I'd like to break our maturation stages into three phases: silly women, women in development, and single wives, which I've already defined.

Silly women have no awareness about the importance of living a life of purpose in God, have no relationship with God and have a life that is completely "out of order", off-centered and disconnected as their spiritual core is not connected to the true source of power for purpose. They live in the moment, doing whatever feels good to them with no regard for the consequences of their actions, which is a key sign of immaturity. These women are living a life according to their own purpose; chasing men, money, or other idols for fulfillment in life and are completely empty on the inside as a result.

As such, they fill themselves with drugs, alcohol, false love or sex to feel better. Since they do not know who they are in Christ, they try to find their identities in the men whom they attach themselves to. They have no life plan, personal or professional goals, or a value system to guide their behavior so they simply live recklessly. Their life is full of the consequences of living recklessly, including having unhealthy relationships with men, married and unmarried. They use their bodies instead of using their brains. They are completely broken inside, and it shows on the outside as evidenced by their low self-esteem, lack of financial grounding or poor parenting skills (if they have children). They consistently involve themselves in dysfunctional relationships with men who are not capable of truly loving them.

Women in development, on the other hand, have matured to the point that they understand that establishing a relationship with God is the key to success and living a life of purpose. They have made the connection to God as their source and are seeking to grow and develop in all areas of their lives, according to good Godly counsel and wisdom. Although they still experience challenges in life, such as making poor decisions from time to time, they quickly get back on track by taking the time to learn from their mistakes so that they will become better women. In addition, women in development have a plan for their lives and are working on achieving their goals to benefit themselves, their families and others. They are destiny-driven, seeking to live at their fullest potential and accomplish all of the great things that God has ordained for their lives. They also may engage in dysfunctional relationships, but if they were given Godly counsel and made aware of the potential effects of their relationship choices, they would be willing to make tough decisions to change their actions to benefit their lives, and their pursuit of love, happiness, health and wholeness.

The ultimate goal is to develop silly women into women in development then into single wives who become married wives. We will explore this idea of single wives and married wives while focusing on the importance of the preparation phase before marriage to assure that your husband finds you prepared for him.

LEARN FROM MY PERSONAL EXPERIENCES

To start our transformation from simply being women to becoming single wives, you must get your mind right. By this, I mean you must address the way you think about love, relationships and marriage. I'd like to offer some advice from my personal experiences that will help you to begin to see yourself, others and relationships from the proper perspective so that you may set standards for yourselves in romantic relationships.

This maturation process starts with overcoming abnormal thought patterns and dysfunctional dating behaviors. I define dysfunctional as "abnormal, impaired or broken down." When we hear the word "dysfunctional" it sounds like a term that is applied to a rare group of people who "really have problems." The fact is that none of us are perfect. We are all impaired or dysfunctional on some level- thus needing to address dysfunctional behaviors. Learn from my past dysfunctional relationship to get an idea of some basic misconceptions that women have about marriage. Hopefully, this will help you to begin thinking about how to make good choices in relationships and prevent heartaches. Below are tips for you if you wish to be married one day.

GET DELIVERED FROM DYSFUNCTIONAL DATING

I was delivered from dysfunctional dating and now I am a certified relationship expert. Allow me to share with you a few of the personal lessons that I learned on my journey that are sure to save you years of frustration, heartache and the pain of making avoidable mistakes. If you have made many relationship mistakes like I have and wish to be delivered from dysfunctional dating, then reading this book will deliver you. If you grasp and apply these concepts in your singleness and in future dating or friendship building, then you will avoid the pitfalls of entering into a faulty marriage covenant and experiencing divorce.

DON'T MARRY FOR THE WRONG REASONS
When I married eight years ago, I was a young Christian girl (I hadn't yet mentally or emotionally matured into a woman) desiring to live right and wanting to not have sex outside of marriage. Although I was not dating a God-led man, I was dating someone who had been a part of my life on-and-off for a significant number of years. We had special chemistry, and we had history. Out of my good desire to be in a stable relationship and begin a family, I basically hurried God's plan for my life because all of my friends and cousins were getting married and having babies. It seemed like I was the only one who wasn't married and pregnant! I didn't possess the fruit of the spirit which includes love, peace, joy, patience, kindness, gentleness, and self-control. Read Galatians 5:22, which explores these aspects of the fruit of the spirit in detail. I was emotionally damaged, unprepared, and completely ill equipped to effectively handle all of the complex dynamics of marriage and unqualified for the job of being a wife at that time.

LEAVE THE PAST IN THE PAST… ESPECIALLY PEOPLE WHO ARE NOT ON YOUR PATH
To be quite honest, the relationship was a dysfunctional childhood courtship that should have remained in my past, but because of various "internal pressures" that I felt during this time in my life, I chose to allow it into my adulthood.

Later, through self-evaluation and reflection, I learned that I made that poor decision because I had unresolved issues with him. I had made a major mistake during our courtship which hurt the both of us deeply. Although I didn't realize this at the time, I felt internally conflicted and sought to "make it right" with him. Additionally, I lacked adequate companionship and support during this voided time in my life; I felt empty, broken and even angry. I was in pain, emotionally, and did not know it. Making a life decision to marry someone at such a vulnerable and sensitive time was not a wise decision.

DO NOT IGNORE SOUND GODLY COUNSEL AND WARNING SIGNS

I ignored wise counsel and the many illuminated warning signs within the relationship that screamed to me, "He is not the one! This is not the marriage that God ordained! Don't do it!" Guess what? I did it anyway, of course.

USE GOOD JUDGMENT-MARRY ONLY COMPATIBLE MATES

I used poor judgment, naturally, and completely flipped the Bible to make it conform to meet my needs and what I had chosen to do for my fleshy benefit. I justified my decision to marry the wrong person by using the excuse that I was trying to do the right thing by God by remaining celibate until marriage. Imagine that. So, I twisted the Bible to make it work for me. At that time, I wanted to do what I wanted to do and not what I needed to do. I needed to have waited to marry when God presented me to the mate that He had prepared for me, instead of one that I had chosen for myself.

At the end of the day, I was trying to fulfill deep voids the best way that I knew how. I also wanted a license to have sex and reproduce. After all, as an accomplished 25 year old living for God, wasn't it time for me to get married and have kids? I mean, we had been together a long time and we "loved each other." Well my friends, love, as we understood it at that time, was not in its purest form, and it wasn't enough to sustain a healthy marriage.

THERE ARE CONSEQUENCES FOR DISOBEYING GODLY INSTRUCTIONS

Neither one of us were prepared for the undertaking of marriage on many levels, but we felt that we were "in love" and that love would compensate for any area of our relational deficit. This was yet another fatal mistake. Looking back, I must say that I was not only living in a fantasy world called denial, but I was also quite delusional.

For some reason, I thought that I could create a husband, that is, completely change a person who did not possess the qualities of a Godly husband and mold them into a husband by my design. I overlooked the facts and accepted a fantasy as truth. I was in a relationship with a person who was not God-led, had no history of being financially stable, and no clear vision and action plan for his Life. So of course he couldn't have one for our life together. He had demonstrated to me during our courtship that he did not understand how to love me appropriately. These warning signs should have been enough for me to come to the conclusion that marriage was not an option for us, but it wasn't. I chose to disobey Godly counsel, disregard past personal experiences and abandon my instincts that screamed that I was not making a wise decision.

I went against my better judgment; became impatient because I was tired of waiting for God's matching process. I wanted to do my own thing based on my own will for my life at that time. After the wedding, the drama was turned up times twenty; the issues that I had experienced with this man prior to the wedding during our courtship, were amplified after the wedding and I had the audacity to cry out and pray that God would help me to "fix" the situation or to turn an ungodly union into a Godly union that would yield fruit. Imagine that!

LIFE EXPERIENCE IS THE BEST TEACHER

Needless to say, the multi-faceted complexities of our dysfunctional union were not fixed. After years of trying to "make it work" despite the many, many challenges, the marriage ended in divorce. I learned countless lessons during the marriage; valuable lessons that would ultimately develop me from being a women in development into a wise woman with a brand new perspective on love and life. I realized how deeply I misunderstood love - even with my best efforts to attract it and give it to others, but through it all, God was with me and showed me love, forgiveness and mercy.

The great thing is the union taught me a lot about marriage. I continued to grow as a person, as a wife, within the situation. I ultimately developed into a strong, mature, and very capable wife before the marriage ended. By the five year mark, I had earned my stripes and definitely qualified for the job as demonstrated by my hard work to evolve. Marriage taught me to be more "we minded" instead of being "me minded" as I was very independent and use to making decisions on my own. It taught me to overcome character flaws such as being demanding and selfish. (Your flaws will be amplified when living with others and being forced to resolve conflicts.) It taught me to develop the fruit of the spirit: love, joy, patience, self-control, kindness, gentleness, long-suffering, etc. It taught me to develop a strong self-esteem and body image to enhance love-making, to develop my wifely skills such as cooking, cleaning and ensuring a welcoming home environment for my family. The greatest gift in it all was learning to perfect and demonstrate Godly love (even when you do not feel like it) within my relationship with my spouse and others. I learned to seek peace at all cost, to love "sacrificially" so that my spouse and others would see Christ in me and so God may get the glory out of my situation and my life. I learned how to forgive, and forgive, and forgive. These are all great gifts that I obtained in a "failed marriage." Therefore, I have learned firsthand that "all things, even our poor choices, bad decisions, and utter disobedience work together for the good of those who love God and are called according to His purpose," as stated in Romans 8:28. This book would not be a reality without my failed marriage and the pain that I experienced in it which pushed me into purpose, and I give God glory!

REALITY CHECK YOURSELF

I reassessed my entire life after my divorce in pursuit of the root causes of my erred judgment as it related to making poor decisions in my past relationships. I began to locate the causes of the misguided thoughts that I had accepted as truths about myself, men and what healthy relationships were supposed to look like. I addressed my low self-esteem and destructive behavior patterns, which led in part, to me passing up many "good men" for the "bad boys." I did the hard work to find out how I had gotten to that place in my life; below ground level, having to start all over after a divorce; losing everything that I had worked hard for - having no money, seeking assistance from countless crisis agencies and churches only to be turned away. I felt completly rejected and alone. Despite my best efforts to display Godly character during extreme marital turmoil, I had been used, abused, neglected, lied to, cheated, mistreated and emotionally trampled on. I really needed some help through this situation and it seemed that I could not get any from anyone, not even the church. I was hurt.

Because of my poor choices, I had lost my home and two vehicles. This was rock bottom for me because I had never been one to ask people for help. I had always worked very hard to be self-sufficient since I left home for college at age 18. I was embarrassed, ashamed and extremely angry with myself for being a fool by putting myself in a situation that caused me to suffer so much unnecessarily.

Even though deep down inside I still had faith that those painful, frightening, and humiliating moments would pass and my future would be much brighter. I knew that I needed to make some real changes in my life immediately. I had to make some serious decisions about my future. The first one was that I would never, ever, allow myself to get into a dysfunctional relationship again,derailing myself away from the path of purpose destiny. I would choose to be single for a lifetime rather to be involved with a man who was an incompatible mate, incapable of loving me, leading our home or treating me with the respect that I'm due as a queen. I would only date men who were husband material.

Another life decision that I made was that I would never be broke another day in my life. I made up in my mind that no matter how hard it was to achieve, I would trust God to see all business visions realized. It seemed impossible to accomplish during the turbulent marriage, but now I would live on purpose and bring to fruition all of the dreams that God had put in my heart. I would give job opportunities and crisis assistance to those who needed them because I knew what it felt like to need help and not be able to get it. I would go hard so that I could become financially capable of supporting myself, parents and other needy family members. I'd build wealth and an inheritance for my future children.

Once I decided those few things, I began to move forward with a vengeance. I took two years off from dating to focus on rebuilding my life, birthing my business and being a student of Christ. I removed myself from the dating market to effectively heal without distraction from the effects of the dysfunctional marriage and subsequent divorce. I learned to love myself, understand my value and worth and develop a deeper relationship with God. I had to purify myself from toxic, negative emotions of anger, bitterness and resentment so that I would not hurt the new mate that God would bring into my life. These basic steps were necessary for my emotional maturation; to adequately prepare me for the next stage in my journey; marriage with my God-ordained mate.

LIFE EXPERIENCE IS THE GREATEST TEACHER

I agree in part that life experience is the greatest teacher. I am thankful for the many developmental lessons learned through making so many relationship mistakes and experiencing a subsequent failed marriage. However, I must admit that I would have preferred not to go through all of the trauma, drama and long-lasting pain that came along with making those poor choices.

As such, I urge you to use this book as a preventive guide to save you years of recuperative training at the "school of the hard knocks," by learning from the lessons that I've provided for you in this book.

INTERNAL PROCESSING AND HEALING

Most experts would recommend that people should take at least six months to one year of personal recuperation and healing time post major break-ups before entering into another relationship. This would be especially true for those of us who have had an extensive history with a partner or experienced a divorce. I used the word devastation to describe the pain of divorce because in divorce, two people who were "one" in every aspect of their lives are essentially breaking apart from each other and becoming two separate individuals again. That is devastating. Depending on the relational dynamics, the simplicity or complexity of the marriage and/or divorce, this could be a life-shattering experience with lingering effects that are likely to affect all future relationships if recuperative assistance is not sought.

LET GO OF UNREALISTIC EXPECTATIONS

There are no perfect people, including you. Although you may have a list of ideal characteristics of your future mate, which you should, don't expect him to be without fault. You should have a vision for your marriage that includes all of the things that you desire, but your mate being perfect should not be an expectation.

We are all working towards perfection, and that journey will not be completed as long as we live on earth. Keeping that in mind, it's such a comfort to be able to be yourself and have a person that is accepting of you with all of your flaws and imperfections. Your God-ordained mate will be this kind of person. While they will accept you for who you are at the present, they will also assist you in growing into the person that you are destined to be. They will support and cover you in your weaknesses while pulling the best out of you. This type of nurturing friendship will give you the confidence necessary to continue growing as a person in a loving and safe support system of an intimate friend.

So, you must understand the mutual implications of having a marriage that provides you with an intimate friendship and firm support system; your future husband will need you to provide the same for him, a safe and nurturing environment so that he may grow in his areas of weaknesses. This support system, the foundation, should be built before marriage occurs though. If you spend the proper amount of time developing a friendship during the dating stage, then you should have a good idea of your mate's personal challenges or weaknesses. If you listen closely to your mate, pay attention to the signs, are prayerful and operating in discernment, things will be revealed to you about your mate; his personality traits, character, life patterns, etc. It will then be completely up to you to make a decision as to whether you will be able to handle (for a lifetime) the reality of the things that are shown to you about your mate.

If you feel that you could not be completely happy with accepting his lifestyle, personality traits, behavior patterns, and other demonstrated indications of character, then you may wish to evaluate the relationship; reconsider him as a potential marriage partner because those types of things do not change after marriage. To think that he will just stop negative habits and adopt completely different values than the ones that he lives by before the wedding is a completely unrealistic expectation. Unfortunately, you will not be able to change him. Sorry, many have tried that and it just does not work. The reality is, a person's personality and character flaws are amplified after marriage as they become more comfortable within the security of the relationship. There is less motivation for them to change after marriage because you are already in a "committed and permanent" relationship. So do not fool yourself; what you see is definitely what you get!

MY JOURNEY TO WHOLENESS

My five-year marriage was so dysfunctional that I don't even know where to begin disseminating all of the relational issues that we had between the two of us. Let's just say that it was heavy on the drama side. I cried a lot, yelled more and we argued a whole lot. We both were very stressed, frustrated and unhappy most of the time. When I wrote out my "little list of good and bad" within the marriage as instructed by Janet Jackson in the Tyler Perry movie, "Why Did I Get Married," the good definitely did not outweigh the bad, which from the movie's advice would indicate my need to seriously re-evaluate my marriage. I truly came to understand what others tried to warn me of before my wedding, "a house divided against itself will not stand" (Mark 3:25). It is difficult to walk with a person when you are both on different paths to completely different locations. The Bible asks us, "Can two walk together unless they have agreed to do so?" (Amos 3:3). The answer is no, they can't.

I learned the hard way what it meant to try to operate in a divided home where the wife carried the weight of leadership and pushed for the husband to submit his life to God so that the family could live according to Godly principles. I was in a situation where I was "unequally yoked;" incompatible, naturally and spiritually, with my spouse, and that made for a tremendous amount of additional relational problems because we were completely out of the God-ordained order for marriage.

When marriages operate out of Godly order; confusion and chaos will be commonplace. Tension, disappointment and frustration will exist between the two incompatible people because they are not usually being allowed to be themselves. They are not getting what they expected from the other person in the relationship and are being pressured to behave in a manner that goes against their true desires. For example, in my case, my partner was frustrated often because he was being pressured to be more spiritual than he really desired to be. He would often go to church because if he did not it would be an issue for us. So, he would usually jump on board to attend spiritual events only because he was trying to resolve conflict between us as opposed to being led from the inside to go. Basically, he just wanted to appease me, or make me happy instead of seeking God out for himself out of his own personal desire to grow spiritually.

I was frustrated because he didn't take the initiative to seek God on his own. I didn't want to have to "beg him" to lead our household based on Christian principles. I did not initially realize that our major differences of beliefs regarding spirituality would make it more difficult for me to serve God within the marriage. I learned by experience that no, a house divided will not stand no matter how badly I wanted it and tried to force it to.

A HOUSE DIVIDED WILL NOT STAND

I tried to honor the commitment that I had made before God. I always believed that marriage was sacred. I was confused, though, and knew in my heart that I had made a mistake from the beginning. A part of me didn't want the people around me to be right or say, "I told you so," so I stayed in the relationship longer than I probably should have to try and prove them wrong. I tried really hard to make it work despite the fact that the relationship was fundamentally broken before we got married. I somehow thought that I could fix the brokenness, that I could change him or mold him into being the husband of my dreams.

If I could just get him saved and sanctified, among other things, then all of our problems would be solved. God could work miracles, right? Well, I still believe that God can and will work miracles, but He can only do what He is invited to do. He will not force Himself on anyone, and I could not force anyone to submit themselves to Jesus if they aren't ready to do so.

I eventually grew tired of carrying the weight of leadership in managing our household; that is not the biblical role of the wife, but it's the husband's role to lead the family. Although women do it all the time, they were not built to bear that type of responsibility alone.

I also grew weary fighting the battles of trying to pull my mate in a direction that he did not really want to go in, as it was emotionally and mentally draining on me.

All the time that I spent pulling and pushing him, I was falling off my own path. I was not free to be the best person that I could be because I was stressed, depressed and emotionally depleted from fighting the daily challenges that crushed my spirit. I was expected to do everything; to give my all, to make all the sacrifices to support my mate, but I had no one to pour back into me, to support me and encourage me in personal pursuits and the things of Christ. Over time, for the sake of the marriage - my partner, I regressed and became someone else. The scary thing was I moved so far from my element that I didn't know who I was anymore. Life had become a cloudy blur. I was unable to see God's vision for my life, which led me into a deep depression. Subsequently, I began to engage in various self-destructive behaviors to attempt to alleviate the pain.

After the divorce, it took me three years to fully complete the process of inner healing, which included intense self-evaluation, deliverance and strategic forgivness to grow myself past the emotional trauma and pain that I had experienced over the previous years. I had to forgive myself and many others, which took a lot of deep heartfelt work and self-sacrifice that most people are not willing to do.

Although the process of healing was hard work and quite painful, the end result was that love was perfected inside of me, and that is a lifetime gift well worthy of my efforts. Once you learn to perfect love in your heart, in which you have a clear understanding of and accept God's love towards you and you learn to love others that same way, you can accomplish any other goal in life easily. I had freed myself from the bondage of bitterness, resentment, and anger. I had chosen to forgive those who hurt me. If I had not, those toxic feelings would have clogged me up and blocked me from receiving my future blessings. I mean, once you let go of negative emotions like regret, resentment, and rejection and learn to consistently forgive any person, who has hurt you, nothing else can conquer you. Perfect love casts out all fear and true love, the love of God, conquers all.

It took me three years of daily focus or intentional self-discovery and development work to fully evolve from being a woman in development into the powerful single wife that I am now. This was a rocky journey, and I got many bruises along the way. As I look back, though, I am so thankful that God turned all of my pain into purpose! God turned all of my bruises, scars and emotional baggage into blessings! Hallelujah!

GOD TURNED MY EMOTIONAL BAGGAGE INTO BLESSINGS

My three-year journey to wholeness was the time period where I really got to know God more intimately as my friend. Through our fellowship, I grew to know Him by His name, El Roi or "The God who sees me." He became the one who really knew what I was going though and understood me better than anyone else. He became the God who comforted me when my pillows were soaked with tears during my divorce transition. He showed me the greater purpose for having experienced so much hurt, rejection, betrayal and emotional abuse in my past marriage. He saw my desire to know Him in His power to transform my life from the pit to the palace. I knew that He had stored greatness inside of me and my best years were yet to come! I was willing to submit to the process of change and that was all God needed to complete it within me. He just needed my willingness and submission to Him to help me get through that dark season in my life. What a friend we have in Jesus, and I was glad to have had Him with me on my journey!

GOD IS MY HUSBAND AND HE IS ALL THAT I NEED, RIGHT?

As a young, unmarried Christian woman, I've committed my mind, body and spirit to God for His use. I've chosen to operate in purpose by using my singleness as a specific time to work diligently for Him in ministry. Simply put, I've dedicated myself to living a life that is pleasing to Him and that gives Him glory. My commitment to Him includes abstinence or celibacy, meaning that I'm now a re-dedicated virgin and will not engage in any sexual activity until the night of my marriage.

I'll admit that this journey of celibacy over the past three years since my divorce has not been an easy one to say the least. If I were really transparent regarding the challenges in dating as a Christian single, I would not have adequate space to document them within this book. I mean, it is one thing if you are a virgin and have never experienced a man sexually, then you may not be as affected by the body's natural craving for more sexual gratification. God help us who have been married for years and experienced sex and love-making with great frequency without any inhibitions! I have an extremely high sex drive, and although the sexual urges have become more manageable over the past three years of abstinence, they definitely haven't gone away.

As a speaker for various women's conferences, singles workshops, and relationship building seminars, I have heard women of all ages, ethnic origins, and socio-economic statuses make ridiculous claims like, "I don't need a man, I got Jesus, and that's enough for me," or "Jesus is my husband, and He is all I need!"

Oh really now? I mean, if you are super-spiritual and always ignore your sensual or fleshy desires, then you may say yes, this is the case, but I would have to disagree with you. We are all human. Don't get me wrong, the statement that God is our husband and He is all that we need is from a spiritual aspect, is accurate as God fully and completely encompasses all that I need to live my Christian life.

God is our Jehovah-Jerah; our Provider. "He supplies all of our needs according to His riches from the glory in the Kingdom" (Philippians 4:19). The reference of God being our husband denotes that He is our primary connection for all that we need within a relationship. He loves us intimately, provides for us, teaches us, leads and guides us away from danger, and He protects us. That is the role of a Godly husband.

God is my husband, but let's be clear: God is a spirit and unifying or fellowshipping with Him can only be done in the spirit, not in the natural. Having said that, God has definitely touched me spiritually in deep and profound ways that I never knew were possible, but He has not touched me physically. Although I am immensely fulfilled when I praise and worship God, I cannot say that I feel that same way when I desire to be touched physically by another person. My senses cannot connect me to God; only faith into the spirit realm can do that. So it is fair to say that at times there is a part of me that is not being engaged as a single woman. I'm in part, voided even though I am in relationship with God. The unengaged part of me would be my erotic or sensual side. This is why I do not agree with the notion that "God is all that I need," because I need to feel the warmth of a person close to me sometimes. I need physical stimulation to engage my sensuality at times. That is a natural innate desire and human need for an intimate, physical, companion.

God gave us senses to enjoy the wonders of this world through sight, smell, hearing, taste and touch. To eradicate our natural desire for sensual stimulation by submerging ourselves in the spirit realm by only focusing on spiritual things would deny our connection with the world around us and our need to interact within it accordingly. Maintaining proper perspective regarding priorities, boundaries, and maintaining natural and spiritual balance in all things are the keys to successfully engaging all parts of our personhood at the appropriate times in life and in relationships. God said it best in Genesis Chapter 2, "It is not good for man to be alone." I agree with Him, as I need physical companionship in addition to my spiritual connection to God.

GOD HELP ME; HOW DO I FIND MY HUSBAND?

I'm sure you have been a part of conversations with women discussing the newest dating options and trying to "find themselves a husband." Well, that would be the first mistake. We, as Godly women, do not find our husbands. We prepare ourselves for them to find us. Under God's direction, this will happen effortlessly in God's perfect timing. The key is preparing for that moment. I submit that we are the ones who delay our divine moments by not being ready to receive the things that we are hoping and praying for.

Although I seldom use the word "dating", as I believe in befriending potential mates and using our time to get to know each other, deeply, before committing to a serious relationship with each other, I will use the term in this book. Dating these days is definitely much different than in times past and the art of finding a spouse that honors God certainly has perplexed many.

God has given us in His Word specific principles concerning what we should look for in a mate. Sadly, too often even Christians are confused in our generation about how to select a marriage partner. Many times this is because they sit under leaders who do not believe or teach that the Bible is a sufficient guide in all areas of our lives. However, the Bible does give ample guidance for all areas of our lives; including instructions in the areas of dating and selecting compatible mates for marriage.

WHAT DOES A GOOD MAN LOOK LIKE?

Psalms 37:23 states that "The steps of a good man are ordered by the Lord and He delights in his way." That would also mean that the converse statement is true. If a man is not walking in the preordained steps of Godly instruction then he is not a good man and the Lord does not delight in his ways.

This is, my friend, the most important factor for you in determining suitability of a potential mate. They must be Kingdom-minded, fully connected to God as their source of power and they should be operating in their Godly purpose.

LOVE IS ALL WE NEED, RIGHT?
You love each other and that's enough to sustain a marriage, right? Wrong! Not so; there are many other integral elements of a successful marriage, one of which is hard work. Marriage requires hard work on a daily basis from both partners; constant self-sacrifice to benefit your partner's needs and submission to the process of personal growth. However, the mutual rewards or fruits from the hard work, in my opinion, are well worth the efforts.

One of the greatest rewards is that marriage provides a safe haven for each person to grow and develop into Christ likeness together. There is a reliable support system that revolves around God. This is the proper foundation where all healthy relationships form and thrive. Love is not enough to make a marriage work. The relationship must be God-centered, as He is true love, and built on spiritual principles, which is the foundation for sustainability and growth.

SUITABILITY
In addition to having love and God-centeredness, healthy marriages require that both people in the relationship are compatible for each other; that they are "suitable" to meet each other's needs within the relationship. The Bible defines a suitable companion as a "help-meet", not help mate. A help-meet is the original Hebrew word for term "helper suitable" or companion in Genesis 2 as Eve was just right and capable of helping Adam to meet His God-given responsibilities of over-seeing or managing the Garden of Eden. A suitable helper will be able to complement you in your God-ordained tasks and help to you meet the demands of life associated with

completing your life assignment or Godly purpose. You need a suitable companion or a "help-meet."

Let's look at the example of God's divine matchmaking with the first marriage couple, Adam and Eve. Remember that I said the definition of single entailed being unique or a special one set apart for exclusive purposes? It also means that you are a good treasure or "one suitable for companionship." Adam was "single" for a while because there were no suitable mates for him in the garden. He was special to God and was of great value. Therefore, God could not place just anyone in his life as that would not help him to fulfill his purpose or remove the loneliness that he felt. I'm a witness that you can live in a house with someone, sleep in the same bed with them, and not be really connected to them and still feel alone. Having just anybody in your life is not the answer to alleviating loneliness. God later said, "it was not good for man to be alone.... I'll make him a helper suitable" or a help-meet. This suitable helper is a companion that is "just right", hand-picked, specially tailored to meet his spiritual, physical, mental and emotional needs.

God understood that man needed human relationship, and He also knew that it could not be just any relationship to fill the void of loneliness. It had to be a suitable companion who would help you and not hurt you. God-ordained relationships will cause each person to draw closer to God and accomplish Godly purpose. The ideal mate must be capable of meeting your deepest spiritual needs and not just your physical needs or you will still feel voided and lonely.

If you read the full story of God's matchmaking process in Genesis Chapter 2, Adam was "single" in the Garden of Eden prior to God creating Eve, but he wasn't alone. God was present, and there were also animals in the garden that Adam was responsible for tending to. Adam had a job; he was given an assignment from God to manage the garden and name all of the animals. All of the animals were paired up two by two with suitable companions, and maybe that caused Adam to start to feel that he needed a suitable companion too!

Similarly, we see others who are paired up and we begin to feel loneliness; this is how it happens in life. This feeling is natural and God even said that He understands. He said, "It's not good for man to be alone," but He doesn't want you to settle and be with just anybody because you are feeling lonely. He wants you operating in purpose while He prepares for you a help-meet that is suitable for you: a companion that is capable of meeting your deepest spiritual and physical needs. That companion, who is just right for you, will be delivered to you at just the right time. God's set time occurs when divine opportunity meets your preparation.

DON'T BELIEVE THE HYPE

With all of the ugly divorce statistics, celebrity break-ups, and the manifestation of so many types of non-traditional relationships, it seems that the media and society are constantly sending us the message that traditional marriages don't work and there are other ways to "be married."

Basically, society would lead you to believe that you don't need to follow the God-ordained marriage pattern but at the same time you should expect to still yield the fruit of a Godly marriage.

No matter what society portrays about marriage, the union is still designed to be a life-time commitment between two people of the opposite sex for the purposes of demonstrating God's unending love for humanity through a covenant relationship that would yield fruit-seed, or Godly children, who would duplicate this model for marriage.

I DON'T WANT TO BE ALONE!

In Genesis 2, after God brought all of His vision for the earth's creation to fruition, He declared that each creation "was good." After marveling at all that He had created, He said, "it is not good for man to be alone, I will make him a helper that is suitable" (Genesis 2:18). Ecclesiastes 4:12 says that "a three-stranded chord is not easily broken," (in adversity) because "two are better than one as they possess double power and ability" (Ecclesiastes 4:9). With suitable help, you can accomplish more in life and conquer more Kingdom territory than you can alone-double power for purpose!

If you marry unsuitable help, you will work directly against God's plan for your life and derail or destroy your destiny. Many men believe that it is not important if they ever get married and thus prolong their decision to do so for years because of the fear of commitment. Other men feel that they just have not come across the "right one" yet. They are enjoying the benefits of being free agents and are not in any rush to find the right one. Only if these guys knew how important finding their wife was. Their wife is the person God designed to help them succeed and fulfill their God-ordained purpose. Life would be much easier for men with suitable help to assist them in accomplishing their goals.

PURPOSE:
ARE YOU WORKING ON YOUR ASSIGNMENT?

Single Wives are unique, set aside or "single" specifically to fulfill special purposes in their singleness. When I minister on the power of purpose, it usually includes much needed teaching on the importance of fulfilling spiritual callings and assignments in life because we all have been created by God to serve a purpose; to do certain things within our earthly lifetime. Do you know what your purpose is? Why you were created? What assignments has God called you to do? Some people associate callings and assignments with only ministerial clergy, but the reality is that we all have specific callings to fulfill in life. Our ability to identify with and actively engage in completing those assignments will directly affect everything else in our lives, including meeting our true marriage partner.

Let's bring our attention to a biblical story of a young lady who by being obedient to her spiritual leadership and following specific instructions got the husband of her dreams, Boaz. If you are not familiar with the Book of Ruth then I encourage you to read it in its entirety. There are only four short chapters in the book, but it provides a powerful example of how operating in Godly purpose automatically places you in the proper position to be identified by your God-ordained mate.

While working on her assignment, Ruth was found and swept away by her rich, handsome and powerful husband Boaz. Boaz came to know about Ruth by hearing about her honorable deeds in the community. People were talking about her commitment, good character and compassion for the needy as she devoted herself to taking care of Naomi, who was a widow requiring special support in her depression. She listened to Godly instruction from Naomi, her spiritual leader, which led her to being in the proper place at the right time to be located by her man!

STUCK ON SINGLE

If Ruth had not been emotionally free, physically available and literally in place for Boaz to find her, she would have missed the divine moment; her appointment to meet her husband. Some women miss their opportunities for destiny because they are resistant to change in one-way-or-another. If you desire to be married and your life is not moving in that direction for whatever reason, it means that you are stuck; stuck on single. The term stuck indicates that there is a resistance to progression or undesired lack of movement. Our lives should always be progressive and accelerating and not stagnant or moving backwards.

Earlier we listed a few reasons for stagnation or regression in areas of relationships, and one of them was emotional bondage. Emotional bondage causes all kinds of negative emotions, such as fear, disappointment, depression, anxiety and low self-esteem. These feelings will prevent us from making ourselves fully available to the possibility of experiencing loving relationships. Please hear me, these feelings will render you ineligible for even the possibility of entering into a healthy and loving relationship because inside, you actually feel that you do not deserve one. As a result, you send signals to those around you that you are unlovable, that you do not want or deserve love and that is exactly how the world responds to you.

We often send off these subconscious and literal messages to others, because of our negative perceptions of ourselves, and the world around us based on our past experiences. The way that we treat others and ourselves is a result of those same experiences, which most often began to take root long ago in unhealed wounds from childhood trauma.

CHAPTER 2: JOURNEY TO WHOLENESS

FREEDOM FROM EMOTIONAL BONDAGE: CHILDHOOD TRAUMA

My definition of "childhood trauma" is any situation, circumstance or personal experience that disrupts a child's sense of safety and security. Basically, it's any life-altering event that leads to long-lasting physical, psychological or emotional damage to the person and ultimately affects how they come to view or perceive the world. Just like the term dysfunctional, childhood trauma sounds like something that affects a "rare" group of people, but the reality is that almost everyone has experienced some type of childhood trauma. Experiencing childhood trauma can have severe and long-lasting effects that flow over into adulthood. This is likely because children who have been traumatized see the world as a frightening and dangerous place and have great difficulty trusting others in general.

When childhood trauma goes unresolved, this fundamental sense of distrust, fear and helplessness carries over into adulthood, thus setting the stage for further trauma, which plays out in our relationships with others subconsciously. We attempt to "relive the pain" from our childhood because that is what is familiar to us. Children who have experienced trauma tend to grow up and engage in what psychologists call, "co-dependent relationships." Webster's dictionary defines co-dependency as "an addiction to people, things, or events." It is the fallacy of trying to control inner feelings by controlling other people. Control, or the lack thereof, is the central theme in the co-dependent person's life.

The definition of co-dependency has changed a bit over time; the original concept was developed to acknowledge the responses and behaviors people develop from living with an alcoholic or substance abuser. However, over the years, co-dependency has expanded into a broader definition, describing a dysfunctional pattern of living and faulty problem solving techniques usually developed during childhood.

Another widely accepted definition of codependency within the therapeutic community is: "a set of maladaptive and compulsive behaviors learned by family members in order to survive in a family, which is experiencing great emotional stress or pain." Maladaptive means the person has an inability to develop behaviors to get their needs met, while compulsive is a psychological state where a person acts against their own will or conscious desires- such as an addiction.

As adults, co-dependent people have a greater tendency to get involved in "toxic relationships," or unhealthy relationships with people who are perhaps unreliable, emotionally unavailable, or needy. The co-dependent person basically tries to provide and control everything within the relationship without addressing their own needs or desires thus setting themselves up for continued disappointment and hurt. This is the dysfunctional pattern that usually continues throughout their lives.

Even when a co-dependent person encounters someone with healthy boundaries, the codependent person still operates in their own system; they're not likely to get too involved with people who have healthy boundaries. This, of course, creates problems that recycle; if a co-dependent person doesn't get involved with a person who has healthy behaviors and healthy coping skills, the problems will continue and carry into future relationships.

Without getting too deep into psychological terminology and theories, here are a few main causes that can lead to emotional or psychological trauma. A few examples include being abused by a parent, being molested or raped, being placed into foster care or adopted, experiencing the divorce of your parents and having a parent who was addicted to drugs or alcohol. Other overlooked trauma stems from ongoing relentless stress, such as living in a crime-ridden neighborhood, suffering from emotional neglect from a parent who wasn't present, living in poverty or witnessing domestic abuse in the home.

Traumatic experiences happen without notice, but could happen repeatedly or in cycles, which in most cases, one feels powerless to prevent them. This is especially true for childhood trauma because children are completely powerless and at the mercy of those who care for them. As such, trauma such as verbal, physical, or sexual abuse at a young age affects people in a very profound way, causing deep-rooted and complex developmental delays and emotional wounds that require specialized attention to heal.

A few emotional effects of trauma are fear, guilt, shame, anger, hopelessness, difficulty concentrating, withdrawal and disconnection from others in relationships. These negative thought patterns are imprinted in the mind. If the earlier trauma occurred in childhood, this would decrease the likelihood that one would be internally healthy enough to attract a healthy partner. I am not saying that all people who have experienced trauma will be affected by the trauma the same way. Some people rebound quickly from even the most tragic and shocking experiences and go on to enter into healthy relationships. This, however, is a rare occurrence.

Starting on the journey to internal healing and recovering from a traumatic event is not easy and takes time. Everyone heals at his or her own pace. Completing the healing process took me roughly three years and there are still areas that I continue to develop and grow beyond, as the past attempts to haunt me from time to time. If months have passed but your symptoms such as feeling of guilt, shame, fear, etc... aren't letting up, then you may need to continue seeking professional help from a trauma expert to help you to work through your feelings more intently.

Here are some basic symptoms of emotional stagnation from trauma that may suggest that additional healing is necessary:

- Having trouble functioning at home or work
- Suffering from severe fear, anxiety or depression
- Inability to form close, satisfying relationships; trusting others is very difficult
- Experiencing terrifying memories, nightmares or flashbacks
- Avoiding things that remind you of the trauma or choosing to live in denial that it did not occur
- Being emotionally numb and disconnected from others; anti-social
- Using alcohol, drugs, sex, or food to feel better, or

demonstrating other addictive behaviors

There is nothing better than getting a solution to your problem and being able to move forward in your life, feeling free and empowered. Professional help provides us with those results. There is nothing weak or silly about seeking professional help, so don't be influenced by others who feel that therapy doesn't help. It is, however, important that the therapist you choose has experience treating trauma or whatever specific area you need targeted therapy in. Choose a therapist that you feel comfortable with. Trust your instincts. If you don't feel safe, respected or understood, find another therapist. There should be a sense of trust and warmth between you and your therapist.

To heal from psychological and emotional trauma, you must face and resolve the unbearable feelings and memories that you've long avoided. Otherwise, those feelings will return again and again, unbidden and uncontrollable. You'll be so glad that you gave yourself the gift of healing and freedom from internal bondage. Take care of yourself, be free to live and love!

SELF-HELP AND RECOVERY TIPS

Although I am a firm believer in seeking professional, secular, assistance from trained therapists who are skilled in counseling techniques to help us understand and apply recovery methods, I also believe that there is a spiritual solution to all earthly problems. The Single Wives Workshops combine these two concepts: the application of natural and spiritual healing methods.

The Single Wives Healing Workshops incorporate both spiritual healing principles to solve the root of emotional issues and therapeutic recovery techniques to assist people to apply spiritual principles and therapeutic recovery methods to their everyday lives. Should you need intensive assistance in the area of inner healing and spiritual deliverance, schedule an one-on-one session, which will provide you with the personal attention necessary to identify and overcome hidden emotional obstacles. These sessions are offered in addition to general workshops for churches, women's groups and various other organizations. Please contact us to host a Single Wives event in your city, or a personal healing and deliverance session via telephone or in person.

The basic self-help tips included in this book will help you in the meantime to begin the healing process and open up to attracting new healthy experiences and relationships. This will be helpful when you prepare to make new friends, that may be potential marriage mates if they are single!

SETTING HEALTHY BOUNDARIES
Emotional boundaries are crucial in helping us to enjoy healthy relationships and to avoid unhealthy or dysfunctional ones. In my opinion, a successful relationship is composed of two mature and emotionally healthy individuals, each with a clearly defined sense of her or his own identity and purpose. Without understanding one's self or what makes you unique, you would probably experience difficulty engaging in an ongoing relationship with another person in a way that is functional and healthy.

We must have a clear sense of self to clearly communicate our needs and desires to another person, specifically our partner. When we have a strong sense of our own identity, we do not feel threatened by the intimacy of the relationship and can appreciate and love those qualities in our partner that make him or her a unique person.

When two people come together, each with a clear definition of their individuality, the potential for intimacy and commitment can be astounding. The commonalities between two people may bring them together, but in an ideal partnership, sometimes called "interdependent," the relationship is mutually beneficial as both partners depend on each other. Their differences are respected and contribute to the development of their relationship—no one carries all of the emotional weight in the relationship, which fosters growth of the individuals in that relationship.

Personal boundaries are the limits we set in relationships that allow us to protect ourselves from being manipulated by or enmeshed with emotionally needy individuals. Such boundaries come from having a good sense of our own identity, value and self-worth. One feature of a healthy sense of self is the way we understand and work with our emotional boundaries. Personal boundaries are the limits we set in relationships that allow us to protect ourselves from being manipulated, used or abused by others.

Healthy boundaries enable us to separate our own thoughts and feelings from those of others and to take responsibility for what we think, feel and do. Boundaries are part of the biological imperative of maturation as we become adults in our own right. Each one of us is unique, and boundaries allow us to rejoice in our distinct identities.

Healthy, intact, boundaries are flexible and allow us to get close to others when appropriate and to maintain our distance when we might be harmed by getting too close. Good boundaries protect us from becoming engulfed in abusive relationships and pave the way to achieving true intimacy with others.

By contrast, unhealthy boundaries are generally formed as a result of being raised in dysfunctional families. In such families, the children were not allowed to properly undergo the maturation and individuation. In these types of families, the unmet needs of parents or other adults are sometimes so overwhelming that the task of raising children is demoted to a secondary role, thus dysfunction is the likely result.

Let's consider the role of a father or mother who screams at their children or becomes physically, verbally or emotionally abusive with them as a self-centered way of dealing with his or her stored up anger or grief. The emotional fallout of these unmet developmental needs, depending on the severity of the original pain, often is close to the surface and can be triggered by totally unrelated present circumstances. The pain of the parent's own childhood experiences repressed for so long are felt again. Insisting that these experiences be dealt with, the present needs of the children for safety, security, respect and comfort are relegated to second place at best.

Sometimes because of the negative self-worth of the parent, the child can be perceived as the "enemy," and the dysfunction is passed on from one generation to the next. This is not to say that the childhood experiences of the parent were necessarily horribly abusive.

What may have been acceptable parenting practices in their family of origin, for generations, may have been abusive. For example, if a female rose in families where there is a social "double standard" for males and females, she will grow to develop misguided concepts about gender roles and possibly her self-worth. As an adult, she'll play these concepts out in future relationships.

An application of this example is a home where the parents give the male children privileges that the female children are not afforded, where the males are able to stay out late, do no chores, are rewarded by the father for their sexual exploits, and do not have to meet academic expectations in school—while on the other hand, the females have strict rules to abide by in the home, must complete all of the household chores, must make excellent grades and are reprimanded if they come home late or have "too many" boyfriends.

These parenting styles and practices are derived in part, possibly, from misguided underlying attitudes about gender roles and socialization of males and females. This sends mixed messages to the children about acceptable behavior of males and females, unbalanced ideas about what they should expect from the opposite sex, and how they should conduct themselves in a family structure, specifically in relationships.

CO-DEPENDENCY

If you can't imagine who you would be without your mate or relationship then chances are you come from a dysfunctional family of origin and have learned co-dependent behavior patterns.

When you lack a sense of your own identity and the boundaries of the self that protects and defines you as an individual, you tend to draw your identity and your sense of self-worth from your partner or significant other.

This is the same process that occurs in the earliest stages of our biological growth in our family of origin. We draw our sense of identify and self-worth from the perceptions that those significant to us had of us. The structure of the relationship, in this case, is not that of equals in a partnership but that of parent and child. Children developing in a family where the important relationship of the parents is an unequal one will be forced to take on roles as either surrogate spouse and/or adopt roles that they hope will restore dignity to the family and balance to the system.

People in co-dependent relationships are unable to find fulfillment within themselves and look for such fulfillment in others. They are usually willing to do anything to make the relationship work just as they may have done in their enmeshed family of origin— even if it means giving up their emotional security, friends, integrity, sense of self-respect or independence. Depending on the complexity of the family dysfunction, the people in co-dependent relationships may even endure objectification – an attitude where they are no longer perceived as feeling like a human being, but rather an object in the family system. They also may endure physical, emotional or sexual abuse just to save the relationship. These are the severe results of experiencing childhood trauma, and the long-lasting effects carry over into adulthood and affect all subsequent relationships.

PERSONAL DISCOVERY AND LIFE LESSONS

I would offer that each of us searches deep within ourselves to find out what makes us unique, then we will rejoice in the freedom of this discovery. We will come to realize that our value and worth as a person is not necessarily dependent on having a significant other in our life, but we can function well as independent people in our own right. When we grow to accept ourselves for exactly who we really are — the good, the bad, and the ugly—we will be able to accept others for who they are as well.

Our relationships and self-confidence actually will have a chance to grow and our emotions will develop past developmental blockages that occurred during moments of past trauma. This will allow us to fully mature as adults who are able to give love freely out of choice and flourish in our new found identity and freedom.

The journey of self-discovery can be both challenging and painful but highly rewarding. Working with a trained minister, therapist or participating as part of a support group can provide the structure and support necessary to complete the process of inner healing of your emotions. But whatever recovery method chosen, the first step is to acknowledge to ourselves, God, and possibly another person that our lives as we have tried to control and manage them have become unmanageable. The second is to give ourselves over to the cleansing and renewal processes. The final step is to stick with it, see it through until you see positive changes like continued happiness, joy, and peace in your emotions and connected with healthy loving relationships.

NEVER SETTLE FOR LESS THAN YOU DESERVE

To believe, for whatever reason, that if you are not experiencing joy, happiness, peace and fulfillment in your relationships that things are good enough as they are is not okay. This would be settling for less than you deserve because you deserve to be loved, cared for, respected, romanced and treated like the queen that you are. You deserve the best of the best in life and happiness as a basic standard of that.

Sometimes we feel a false sense of security in particular relationships that have been challenging and begin to feel that we don't deserve any better. We start to feel that helping others is the most important element in our relationship; self-sacrifice is noble, and that's as good as it gets. This is simply untrue. Helping others is noble, but it is also noble to help yourself. Life and our relationships should be progressive, always getting better and better as we grow and expand our capabilities to love and experience love.

When we settle for less than the best by choosing mates that are not capable of recognizing our worth and treating us with dignity, respect, and love, then we give up the chance to be the person we were meant to be, and are not able to explore our true sense of personal fulfillment in life. When we give up our personal life dreams and sense of self-worth to maintain the happiness of someone else, then this is a dysfunctional relationship.

A healthy relationship is one in which boundaries are strong and flexible enough to allow us to flourish with our own uniqueness. These boundaries are known and respected by each person in the relationship. There is a sense of respect on the part of both partners that allows each person to live as full a life as possible to explore their own personal potential. Anything less than this would be settling for less than the best and ultimately giving up ourselves for the sake of a potential relationship.

GUILT AND MISAPPROPRIATION OF RESPONSIBILITY

Another characteristic of growing up in a dysfunctional household is that you may learn to feel guilty if you fail to ensure the success and happiness of other members of the household. You may feel responsible or be made to feel directly responsible for the failure or unhappiness of others as a child.

Consequently, in adulthood, you may come to feel or be made to feel responsible for our partner's failures. The guilt that you feel when your partner fails may drive you to keep tearing down your personal boundaries so that you are always available to help the other person. When you feel the pain, the guilt and the anger of being overly responsible for another person's behavior or life experiences, you may seek to alleviate their negative feelings by rescuing them from the consequences of their behavior, as we learned in our family of origin. Within the therapeutic community, this is called enabling behaviors.

ENABLING BEHAVIORS

Enabling behaviors gives power; authorize or assist a person to engage in particular behaviors that are generally destructive in nature. Examples include giving a person money to buy drugs or alcohol, paying an adult's bills when they are fully capable of working to support themselves but won't, and making excuses for their poor behavior rather than confronting them in love to assist them to make positive changes in their lives and take responsibility for their actions. When you enable a person, you actually stunt their growth or maturation process.

Over the years in both my personal relationships and professional life, I've seen quite a number of enabling behaviors exhibited between mothers and their sons in family structures. For various reasons, the mothers tended to inappropriately parent their sons by not giving them tough love when necessary. They often "co-sign" on negative behaviors by not instructing their sons effectively on how to "grow up" and conduct themselves as mature men in relationships. They would cover up for them when they got in trouble with the law, mistreat females in relationships, act irresponsibly with money, and failed to parent and provide for their children. The familiar nickname, "mama's boys" would effectively describe these types of males.

More detail regarding enabling behaviors between mothers and sons would be, a mother not encouraging her 27-year-old son to maintain employment by paying his bills for him, managing his home affairs, and supporting children that he has fathered but fails to support himself. The son makes poor choice after poor choice and looks to mom to bail him out each time, so he never experiences the consequences of his actions. By depriving her son of experiencing the consequences of his actions, his growth is stunted, and he begins to expect this type of "support" from other women in his life. He ultimately fears managing his own life without help. He will question his ability to make his own decisions in life, which is a necessary part of maturity, manhood and leadership especially if he desires to become a future husband. If this dysfunctional behavior pattern is not addressed, it will spill into the son's romantic relationships, and his mother, unfortunately, is likely to be very involved there as well.

Instead of choosing to enable our loved ones, a healthier response for people in relationships is to show others respect by allowing them to succeed or fail on their own terms. You, of course, should support your children's or partner's fulfillment of their life goals, but it is unhealthy to rescue them from experiencing life challenges that come along with pursuing their dreams.

In romantic relationships, this may be a bit more of a difficult concept to grasp if we have confused love with rescuing others from pain in life. You can be there to help, comfort, or encourage your partner in difficult times without rescuing them. When boundaries are healthy, you are able to say, I trust and respect you to make your own life choices and accept the consequences of your decisions. As my equal partner, I will not try to control you by taking away your choices in life or rescuing you from the consequences of your choices by enabling behavior.

Sympathy and compassion are worthy qualities, but they can be confused with love, especially when boundaries have become distorted or are virtually nonexistent. Healthy boundaries lead to respect for one another and equality in a relationship. There is also an appreciation for the aliveness and strength of the other person and a mutual flow of natural feelings between the two partners. When one partner is in control and the other is needy and helpless, there is no room for the give-and-take or mutual fulfillment, which occurs in a mature and healthy relationship.

FACE THE FACTS

Children from highly dysfunctional households often feel that things will get better someday and that a "normal" life may lie in the future. Indeed, some days things are fairly "normal," but then the bad times tend to return again and again. It's the normal days that give the false sense of hope that all problems in the family might someday be solved. This is a common cycle in highly dysfunctional families.

When children in these families grow up, they carry the same types of fantasy into their romantic relationships. They may portray to others the myth that they have the perfect relationship, and they may even believe deep inside that someday all of their relationship problems will somehow be solved, even without a plan of solution or third-party assistance. Abuse, manipulation, imbalance and control in the relationship are generally ignored.

By ignoring the problems, they are unable to confront them, and the fantasy of a happier future never comes to pass. Issues that are never confronted will never change. We must face the facts and identify when we are living in a fantasy verses reality. Healthy boundaries allow us to test reality rather than rely on fantasy.

ACTION TIPS ON YOUR JOURNEY TO EMOTIONAL HEALING

Isolation is not the answer: Connect with other positive individuals and ask for support. It's important to talk about your feelings often with a trusted family member, friend, counselor or clergyman. In addition to talking often about your feelings in a safe environment, you should strategically connect with positive people, effectively use your time, and not allow yourself to be isolated. Below are a few tips on how to accomplish those goals:

- Participate in social activities. Even if you don't feel like it, do fun things with other people,—go exercise, walk around the mall and window shop – do things that have nothing to do with the traumatic experience. Change your environment often. If you've retreated from relationships that were once important to you, make the effort to reconnect. Check online for free community events in your area and just go.

- Join a support group. Being with others who are facing similar challenges can help reduce your sense of isolation and hearing how others cope and have overcome, can help inspire you to have hope for a better future.

- Volunteer. Helping others can be a great way to challenge the sense of helplessness that often accompanies trauma. Remind yourself of your strengths and reclaim your sense of power by comforting or helping others. Sow healing into the life of another person, and you'll be surprised at the miraculous effects of healing that return into your own life.

- Create a daily routine. Following structured schedules help you to stay grounded after a trauma. Set regular times for waking, sleeping, eating, working and exercising. Make sure to schedule time early in the morning for quality time with God, expressing thanks to Him for your healing, even when you don't feel it yet. Also, do comforting things for yourself such as just relaxing, getting a massage, or treating yourself to a gift of your choice. Social activities are great, have fun!

- Don't take on too much. Break large jobs into smaller, manageable tasks. Take pleasure from the accomplishment of achieving something that you have set out to do. Achieve even the smallest goal that you have made for yourself this will have enormous positive effects on your self-esteem and confidence.

- Increase your personal value. Invest in yourself while keeping your mind occupied. Idol minds are the devil's workshops. Use your time to learn a new skill, sharpen your intellect and improve your body image. Knowledge is empowering. Read a book, take a class or learn to cook new dishes. Exercise and go through your closet to revamp your image by selecting new styles for yourself. When you look better you feel better!

- Allow yourself to feel what you feel when you feel it. Denial is not the answer and pushing things under a rug "not to deal with them" will not make them go away. Those suppressed emotions will manifest themselves in the form of sicknesses, diseases, addictive behaviors and dysfunctional relationships. Acknowledge your feelings about past traumas as they arise; accept them and deal with the feelings. Accepting your feelings is part of the grieving process and is necessary for adequate healing.

IDENTIFYING HIDDEN ROAD BLOCKS TO ATTRACTING TRUE LOVE

I've learned in my decade plus of facilitating direct mental health services, developing family intervention programs, and providing ministerial counseling to people of all ages and from various walks of life, that lots of people are being tormented by negative emotions. They are struggling daily and seem to be in bondage to fear, anxiety and depression. These are people who are inside and outside of church communities both in the pews and in leadership. Honestly, I've found that the "church people" seem to be the most bound by depression and fear-based attacks.

I'll continue to impress upon you the need to be real with yourself and face the facts about where you are in relation to being emotionally whole. Not dealing with negative emotions will keep you bound, and you will never experience the fullness of life and the true love that you desire– even if you are currently in a relationship or marriage. The inability to resolve or grow beyond emotions or feelings we have in connection with stressful events and circumstances in life can lead to serious depression. Clear your emotional closet by cleaning out undesired negative emotions, destructive habits and any additional stresses. Having a "stinking," cluttered, and clogged up life – chaos on the outside – is a result of not cleaning unresolved emotions and other dirt from the inside. There is no room for new things to enter your life if you are full of dirty toxics-or negativity. This would include the relationship that you are waiting for, as there is no room for King Charming in your life with a closet of internal clutter, which spills over and dirties up your surroundings. Clean house! Both inside and outside.

FEAR BLOCKS FAITH ACTION

The fear of failure is perhaps the strongest force holding people back from living their God-ordained potential. In a world full of uncertainty, a failing world economy, and countless misfortunes and evils that could happen to anyone at anytime, it's easy to see why most people are led into believing that they are in a hopeless situation and doubt that God's Word will come true for them. If you never dare to fail, you can never really succeed. Failure is a very real part of achieving success. Some of the most successful people have experienced a great deal of "perceived failures" before arriving at what others define as sustainable success. Don't be afraid to take chances in life—especially in relationships.

BREAK BEYOND THE BARRIER OF FEAR

I am a personal witness to the fact that while fear is powerful, faith action is more powerful. As an entrepreneur and visionary of a faith-based community outreach organization, I've experienced countless episodes of what I considered as failure after failure after failure, and it can be quite mentally paralyzing. But I've learned that the greater the vision, the greater the associated adversity and potential risks for failure. These are real aspects of attempting to accomplish something great.

Don't get me wrong, I'm a person of extreme faith. Despite the cycles of intense demonic opposition and internal and external forces of adversity working against my progress, I never stopped believing God's Word. I've never stopped trusting in His power working through me, but it was the fear voices of the enemy, and many others around me for that matter, that started to make an impression on my mind. The negativity began to stagnate my growth, as I grew weary in fighting the good fight of faith at times. People are not always happy about your growth and will say negative things or speak word curses over you. When people speak failure over your life, business or relationships, these are curses and you should never underestimate the effects of them. The reality is, failures, negativity and fear can be extremely helpful in assisting us to succeed by pointing out areas of our deficiencies or weaknesses that need improvement. It's all about how you perceive your situation and process past failures and the negative voices of others. You must use everything as ammunition, positive and negative emotions, to move forward despite negativity as a stronger and wiser person who is more capable of achieving your goals.

I decided to use fear as fuel – The moment I decided to succeed in spite of fearful emotions derived from past failures and the negative words of others who enjoyed seeing me "down," they eventually motivated me to succeed all the more. I never gave up or fainted in the adversity but kept growing in faith and never let go of God's vision for my life. That is true success.

I began to silence the voices of the nay-sayers through spiritual warfare. I had to break the word curses and spells that they had spoken over my life, my businesses, my ministry and even my future marriage. Because of my divorce and all of the drama involved in that relationship, some people felt that I would never experience a healthy or successful marriage. Thankfully, they do not have the last say; God does, and He has good plans for me,— plans to bless me, give me hope, and bring me to an expected end (of success) (Jeremiah 29:11)!

You must take this same approach in dealing with your fears and foes to your success by having the courage to follow your passions and execute God-ordained assignments despite the presence of fear. When I did, that's when God responded, and I began to see immediate recovery and miraculous open doors in business, harvest of seeds sown in ministry, and new successful romantic relationships (smile). This book is a seed of faith, as I continue to stand on Ecclesiastics 7:8 that says, "Better is the end of a thing (a situation, story, experience) than the beginning." The faithful inherit the promises!

Revelations 12:11 says, "We overcome by the blood of the lamb and by the words of our testimony!" Although I still experience moments of sadness, loneliness, and anxiety during my marriage preparation phase, I'll continue to testify of God's greatness and past victories in my life to see the manifestation of the promises that I've yet to see materialized.

MOVE FORWARD AND CONQUER

To completely break free from fear, you must take action. For example, those who have a fear of flying should take steps to book a flight and execute those plans. It is the same process with overcoming the fear of failing in relationships. You must begin to take steps to prove that the voices of fear are wrong by moving forward towards destiny despite how you feel. Go out and meet new people, mingle, and have fun in the atmosphere with guys you consider to be ideal mates.

Consider the following when you feel fearful in creating a dynamic vision for your next relationship and marriage: Write the vision and make it plain (Habakkuk 2:2). Then take faith actions by stepping out to expand your horizon by meeting new people who possess the qualities that you would desire in an ideal marriage mate.

The following mental strategies will help you take faith actions by writing the vision for your future relationship; be clear about what you want and add all of the intricate details that you envision, like the description of your future life with your husband, your wedding ceremony, decorations in your home, locations for yearly vacations, names of your children and any other things that you want to have or experience in your marriage. Envision how your future mate will show you love, romance you, and care for you. Envision how fulfilling it will be and how much happiness you will feel.

Here are a few other actions to help you to move forward in faith:

- Seriously consider the cost of missed opportunities. The biggest cost that people fail to consider when they allow fear to paralyze them from moving forward is that they will miss opportunities and experiences they desire. Taking high risk to pursue all potential possibilities is essential in life because the greater the risk the greater the reward.

- Big visions, require big risks to pursue them. Write down your vision for the type of relationship that you desire and pursue it. There is nothing wrong with desiring a man with specific qualities. My vision includes a husband with intelligence, good looks, and wealth in addition to the basic Godly characteristics that I require as a minimum. You miss the opportunity of having things simply by not desiring. "Delight yourself in the Lord and He will give you the desires of your heart" (Psalms 37:4). What are your true desires?

- Explore the Unknown. Go places that you have

never gone before; explore new foods, cultures and diverse people. For example, if you desire a wealthy man, you need to become familiar with how wealthy people live. Where do they eat? What things do they enjoy for leisure? What are the etiquette rules for the wealthy in social settings? The unknown is a major source of fear. When you know what to expect and prepare for where you wish to go, it takes the fear away from going there. You must go places, in your mind, before you literally go places, then you can honestly say to yourself, "I've been here before, so I need not be afraid."

• There are no losses in pursuing your dreams. I would rather pursue my dreams and fall flat on my face than to never try at all. This is because, if you fail, you can get up, learn from it, and keep moving forward to the next experience. This will motivate you to always keep trying, keep moving, and you will eventually obtain exactly what you are after if you don't give up on your dreams. Conversely, you will obtain nothing if you go after nothing.

• Understand the benefits of failure. Failures are like experiments that yield important data for your use to help you succeed in the future. Failures are life experiences that do not define you. You are not your failures. The more failures that you experience, the greater the opportunities to succeed the next time that you try if you learn from the failure. Even if a failure costs you financially or emotionally, the educational benefits that you obtain from learning and applying what your learned in the future far outweigh the losses.

- Don't just talk about it, be about it! The best way to reduce fear and build self-confidence is to take action towards achieving your relational goals. As soon as you do, you'll begin accumulating more experience and knowledge. Everything is hardest the first time. It's like jumping off a cliff into a lake, although I do not advise this, after you've done it once, you'll see that the water is safe and each time afterwards is easier. If you have a relationship goal, but are afraid to follow-through, force yourself into action by not just talking about it, but actually committing to it.

IDENTIFYING WHAT LOVE IS NOT—LOVE IS NOT ABUSE

As women, we are typically wired to nurture, help and to "mother" others, sometimes to the point where we may forget about our own needs to be nurtured, protected and loved. We often overlook the warning signs of abuse in relationships by thinking that abusive behavior is acceptable because we feel that we can help the abuser learn to love us with time. No one deserves to be mistreated, hurt or abused in relationships. While you may think that your boyfriend or husband is just "hot-tempered" or just "stuck in his ways," his actions may be giving you clues to something more.

Our society and the media often flood us with images of dysfunctional relationships, and we come to believe that the dysfunction is normal because we see it so much. For example, we see women who are treated as sex objects and not respected by their partners, and it is accepted by the women in the relationship, so young girls come to believe that they have little value.

A few examples of abusive behaviors that are often dismissed by women in relationships would be having a man who dishonors her by treating her like a door mat, a sexual object or a brainless servant. Others would have a man who holds double standards for himself in the relationship – his feelings matter but hers do not, he enjoys privileges that she cannot, or he is unfaithful, and does not keep promises to her.

I remember a situation in my past marriage that speaks to this type of emotional abuse. Basically, my former partner had his own set of marriage moral rules for himself as the man in the relationship and expected me to perform or conduct myself by a higher standard. He would lie, stay out late, engage in inappropriate relationships with other women, and felt that his reasons for his poor behavior were acceptable time and time again. I, on the other hand, could not "get away" with making those types of mistakes in the relationship and definitely could not "excuse away" those types of behaviors as he often did.

After being caught in various lies on a particular occasion, let's just say there was some really "heated discourse", we were no longer residing at the same residence, and he brought in many people to help him to seek resolution in our marriage. His mother, being one, called me to "plead his case", relay his regret, and vouch for his "love" for me. One of her responses to my unwavering desire to move forward without her son in my life (because consistent disrespect should not occur if he really loved me), was that, "He really loves you, and you know it – see how miserable he is without you in his life? He has made lots of changes for you– it just takes men a bit longer to learn than women – men are just that way and we as women just have to accept some things (disrespectful and abusive behavior) in a marriage." Can you say the devil is a liar? I do agree that some things you do have to learn to accept in marriage, but I don't believe that continual disrespect, dishonesty and unfaithfulness are those things. Now I had been with this guy for a while off and on in my late teens-early twenties and it was a process to finally break free from the cycle of emotional abuse that he inflicted on me. I had accepted him back into my life so many times previously even though he demonstrated to me that he was dishonest. That was my fault. Although I believe everyone deserves a second chance, (a third chance even), when you start giving fourth, fifth, and sixth chances only to be disrespected again, it may be an indication that there are some serious developmental attention needed by both people in the relationship. If these things are not effectively addressed during dating, they are likely to spill over into your marriage and that is not what you want.

People learn how to treat you by the standards that you set in relationships, the boundaries that are demonstrated, not just spoken. No one will do anything to you that you do not allow to be done. His mother obviously had a part in teaching her son that being a dishonest and irresponsible man was "acceptable" in her parenting as she did not take a stronger stand against his poor behavior in the past, which demonstrated that she had self-esteem issues of her own. With much self-evaluation, I finally "really" realized that his behavior was hurtful and unacceptable. I deserved someone to be honest with me and to demonstrate their love to me– not just talk about it or make empty promises. So I left the marriage.

In order for me to assist you in identifying healthy relationships, exploring what unhealthy relationships look like would be helpful. Let's examine typical signs of unhealthy behavior patterns often exhibited in abusive relationships.

PSYCHOLOGICAL ABUSE

Psychological abuse occurs when one's feelings, thoughts, preferences, desires, needs, appearance, or friendships are trivialized or made to appear inconsequential relative to the abuser. In other words, the abuser constructs the rules in the relationship and the world of the victim according to his terms-/conditions over that of the abused for his own gratification, which are often simply control tactics.

Psychological abuse is often overlooked and even dismissed by many women because of confusing societal beliefs about gender roles what should be expected from a man or a woman in relationships. Let's use my previous example of the episode that occurred during my past marriage. I had confronted my mate about a recent act that I considered a personal violation of our trust and breach in the negotiated terms of our marriage.

Although I continuously expressed my feelings, thoughts, and needs to him within the marriage, he in essence dismissed them by continuing to violate my desires and trivializing the importance of my feelings by continuing the hurtful behaviors and justifying them when they were brought up in discussion. Basically, he felt that he could operate by a different set of rules within the marriage than me. He would do things that were unacceptable for me to do "as a Godly wife." He would often brush off his "mistakes," which caused me great pain and brought conflict into the marriage, by giving justifications like, "it was a simple mistake – you are blowing this out of proportion," or, "I just wasn't thinking correctly…you got to understand, men don't always think like women do." What confused me was that as we continued to talk, he admitted that if I had committed the "mistakes" that he had in our marriage, if the tables were turned, then he would be extremely hurt and not likely to forgive me. He still maintained, though, that he deserved another chance in the situation. Hmmmm?

The fact is that some men are stuck in their ways and are resistant to change doesn't justify their poor behavior. Abuse is abuse, and no woman deserves to be mistreated, violated, devalued, dishonored, disrespected and consistently hurt in any relationship. Abuse is not normal – it is not behavior that we should accept from anyone. We are too valuable and deserve to be treated exceptionally well– with love. On my journey to wholeness, I had to learn to forgive my ex and myself for the failures of the relationship. I had unrealistic expectations in the first place, so all of what I experienced was not just his fault. I should not have expected to receive true love from a man who had not connected to the love of God, did not know what true love was, or know how to appropriately give it to a woman. I had to come to the realization that I was very much at fault for lots of things that took place in the marriage too; I was immature, misguided, broken and deficient in my love capabilities too; I mistreated him in many different ways- I hurt him, and we both had "issues." We did the best that we could in the marriage, given the knowledge that we had at the time. None of what he did meant that he was a bad person, it just meant that he was underdeveloped relationally, and thus was not an ideal marriage mate at the time. He is a good person, but not necessarily a good husband for me.

EMOTIONAL CAPTIVITY

Abusers hold power over the abused partner by resorting to a number of tactics designed to keep her emotionally captive. To this end, the abuser may lavish the abused with flattery and praise or compliments that make her feel remarkably indebted to him for the special and often overly generous attention.

At the same time, the abuser may make the abused feel like she is the only one who really "understands him". She is special to him. Unfortunately, her significance to his well-being becomes a weapon that he uses against her later. This becomes evident when she tries to leave the relationship; he may then try to hold her emotionally hostage by positioning her as an ungrateful person for not taking into consideration the special attention given to her or his great efforts to make her happy. He then may make it seem as if the abused is being hurtful to him by trying to "abandon" him as she is the only person in whom he can confide in or get support from.

ESCALATING CONTROL

If she seems to be growing beyond his grip, he may then resort to more sinister control strategies. He may then place his well-being or his very life in her hands. He may begin to threaten to hurt himself or even commit suicide if she leaves him. She now feels overwhelmingly responsible for his welfare and succumbs to his demands for a purely exclusive relationship. He then becomes more prone to using negative and upsetting control strategies to maintain his grip knowing that his threat of self-harm is now all that is necessary to maintain her compliance.

THE EFFECTS OF ABUSE
She sinks deeper and deeper into fulfilling his needs, and her career, family life or personal identity suffers. Anxiety and depression sets in. He toys with her and the relationship, and his emotions can be off and on at his own whim. He can cheat, lie, and manipulate, and she is stuck with it unless her leaving gives rise to his threat of self-harm or "not being able to make it without her."

ESCAPE IS A DECISION AWAY
Escaping such abuse will likely require counseling but can occur without it. Counseling is aimed at helping the abused cognitively step back and process the situation so that she may come to understand the nature of the relationship, the abuse and how she got there. Further, counseling will be aimed at providing tools or strategies to help her extricate herself from the relationship even in view of the threats of harm imposed by the abuser toward himself or her. In other words, counseling is aimed at releasing the abused as hostage and helping her develop better boundaries to withstand the psychological manipulations of the abuser.

EMOTIONAL ABUSE IS ABUSE
I've heard many women dismiss the fact that verbal or emotional

abuse is equally "abusive" as physical abuse. I would argue that emotional or verbal abuse is even more harmful or "abusive" than physical abuse because of the piercing power of words – curses, and their long-lasting effects on a person, which are often still there long after bruises from physical abuse have faded away.

Emotional abuse is a consistent pattern of behavior that results in the eventual demolition of another person's identity; psychological, emotional or physical well-being. Emotional abuse includes a variety of controlling tactics, together with manipulative techniques and strategies. Emotional violation is inherent in every act of incest, rape and physical assault as well as with all other "forms" of abuse. Emotional abuse is as damaging; but since there's no physical trail, the victims or survivors feel completely isolated. The unspoken social dismissals of emotional abuse combined with the internal scarring and pain of the abuse itself are two factors that make emotional violence so traumatizing.

The frustration of emotional abuse exists in part because the victims know they're in pain, but usually can't put their finger on why. They're in a relationship and their partner is sending them mixed messages. For example, your mate expresses his desire to be with you, promises love and affection and other times shows an utter disinterest in the relationship or fails to follow through on his promises to you. When the victim tries to connect with his promise of love, she crashes into a glass ceiling or brick wall. She feels battered, bruised, and broken but can't find the cause.

Emotional abuse is a psychological technique of control and manipulation defined by deception. When you're struck by a 2x4, you are fully aware that you have been hit and know exactly what hit you. When the blow is delivered by a lie or worse, yet a lie disguised in the wrappings of love, then you're left thinking you're the problem. My position is that no one, in any circumstance, should have to endure control, coercion, manipulation or abuse of any kind as that is not love – it is abuse. Having someone tell you that they love you but treat you like a dog is hurtful, confusing, frustrating and deceptive – this is the nature of psychological and mental abuse.

Mental abuse leaves you with many internal emotional conflicts and deep-rooted wounds. A few of the major wounds are the fear of change, a distorted view of love and low self-esteem, which all affect your interactions in future relationships if not addressed properly prior to.

BREAK THE PATTERN OF DATING ABUSIVE MEN

Women who get involved with abusive men are typically those who had abusive childhood home environments. This kind of upbringing tends to normalize abusive behavior in all relationships. What this means is that women from this kind of a background are not as keen on identifying the subtleties of abuse the way "healthy" women are.

There is hope for us who have been involved in abusive relationships because all behavior can be relearned. This includes the ability to recognize early signs of abuse as unacceptable behaviors in a relationship. Once this is learned, you will be able to break free from unhealthy relationships with men who are no good for you. I have listed below a few common abusive behaviors for you to watch for and avoid in relationships; you should pay close attention to the following warning signs that you may be involved with an abusive man and act accordingly. You may be dating an abuser if the man that you are dealing with is a man who:

- Criticizes you about your positive qualities or mocks your accomplishments and calls you names like "goody two shoes," "Ms. Perfect," or "Ms. High & Mighty."

- Has been an abuser in past abusive relationships including verbal abuse; he calls you names like stupid, fat, ugly, lazy, "nothing without him," crazy or emotionally unstable.

- Engages in criminal activities of violence or has in the past.

- Is an alcoholic, drug addict or presents other addictive behaviors.

- Is extremely irritable or has mood swings that result in your feelings being hurt.

- Dismisses your intelligence and discourages your successes or pursuits your dreams.

- Doesn't listen to you, devalues your opinions, or makes you feel stupid for voicing your thoughts, and makes light of your concerns or feelings.

- Is jealous and demonstrates insecurity when you innocently talk to or about other men.

- Has grown up in an abusive family; witnessed abuse of parents, siblings or close family members.

- Is controlling; attempts to keep you from spending time with friends and family, dictates how you should spend your money (some men don't even allow women to have the money that they make), where you go, who you should be around and gives you a curfew.

• Is disrespectful towards you publicly or privately; calls you out your name or makes fun of your weaknesses in front of others or privately.

• Violates your rights to make decisions for yourself and your body; forces himself upon you sexually.

• Is irresponsible and leaves you to solve problems that were created by his irresponsible actions. He blames everyone else for his behavior.

• Persistently lies to you; makes promises and doesn't follow through.

• Starts arguments when confronted about his negative behavior; throws off and becomes the victim himself, or is highly reactive when confronted about his behavior; may get loud, curse, or act out irrationally.

• Have streaks of meanness or aggressiveness towards you and others for no reason.

• Threatens you verbally or with threatening body posturing; pushes, hits, kicks, slaps, restrains, snatches or shoves you for any reason, and it may happen once or repetitively.

• Makes vulgar (sexual) comments about you or other women publically or privately; openly expresses interest in other women in your presence (starring at women or making mention of their attractiveness and admiring their body)

• Compares you with past partners and makes it clear that you do not measure up. Admires other women but never compliments you.

• Makes you feel tied down, stuck or bad about yourself in general; withholds affection or communication with you or disagrees with you or disapproves of your actions.

• Threatens to hurt himself, you or others if you leave him.

To recognize early abusive signs, you must stop rationalizing "abusive" behaviors as "normal." If you see ONE abusive behavior, regardless of how small, you need to remind yourself that it IS abuse. Period! With this new skill, you will soon be dating men who treat you with dignity and respect, which is normal—the way all women deserve to be treated.

Abuse has many effects, but here are a few to watch out for in yourself and others so that you may help them to heal from them. You must overcome the following before you are able to thrive in a healthy relationship:

• Loss of personal drive and motivation or enthusiasm for life

• Self-critical fears about how you are coming across to others expressively

- A concern that something is wrong with you
- Destroyed personal identity and loss of self-confidence
- Feelings that you should not really be happy or that it's acceptable to be unhappy
- Fear that you are "crazy," unstable, overly emotional, or too sensitive
- Feelings that time is passing you by and you are missing out on life
- Hesitancy to accept your own perceptions, emotions, and ability to voice them openly
- Indecisiveness, distrust in men, and perception that all men will treat you poorly
- Hopelessness relating to future relationships or potential future relational bliss

WORDS DO HURT

Can words hurt as much as the bruises of physical abuse? For anyone who has been subjected to a never-ending stream of put-downs and derogatory comments, the effect of those words are just as bad as being hit. The words hit hard, sting and cut deeply—they take root on the inside and grow like a virus with watering of more hurtful words. You see, verbal abuse has a way of wearing down a woman's core, her self-esteem, until she gets to the point of believing the words that have been spoken to her. No matter how pretty she is, she starts to believe that she is ugly, worthless and that nobody else would want her or "put up with her." Even if the person inflicting these verbal wounds claims that he didn't really mean it when he said it, the damage has been done and it accumulates in her heart over time.

In cases of verbal abuse, the man will usually make you feel that you are just too sensitive or that he really didn't mean to hurt your feelings; you just "took it the wrong way." It is as much as what you say to a person and how you say it. If something that someone said to you hurt you, then accept that those were your feelings. Do not let another person dictate how you should feel. Own your feelings and then make the rules for what you will and will not allow other people to say to you in relationships. You set the bar for how you are treated.

TIME DOES NOT HEAL ALL WOUNDS

I cannot repeat enough how badly harmful words hurt and harm a woman's self-esteem. Now imagine that this hurtful cycle continues over several years. The woman tries everything to mold herself into what she believes her husband really wants but it never makes a difference and she never feels loved. Eventually, she becomes a shell, void of untruths, believing that she'll never be good enough, smart enough or pretty enough to please her husband or any other man for that matter.

Keep these things in mind as you meet men and begin to date. At the first sign of put-downs or degrading remarks, you will need to address the situation. Based on the response you get, you must decide if you need to cut your losses and move on.

Unfortunately, nothing that you say or do will change him if he doesn't initiate the change. It is unlikely to be resolved without third-party guidance to get to the root of his dysfunctional behavior; ultimately it's an issue of control. The thing is, many women who have experienced verbal or psychological abuse never viewed themselves as victims of abuse until things turned physical. Unfortunately, verbal abuse often escalates to physical abuse as the abuser seeks more control.

THE EFFECTS OF LIES, REJECTION & BETRAYAL IN PAST RELATIONSHIPS

If you ask any women if she has ever been lied to, cheated on, rejected or betrayed in a romantic relationship, the answer is usually a resounding YES. What is it about finding out that your mate has been unfaithful to you that unlocks the floodgates of emotion? Most women would say that the betrayal, perceived rejection, deception and the humiliation catapults them into an emotional abyss where feelings of despair and sadness alternate with feelings of anger and rage at any moment.

When and if the shocks subsides, the focus of the betrayed woman's thoughts remain on the sexual act mainly because it exemplifies the violation of a sacred trust between two people who have made a commitment to each other. This type of hurt from an affair causes a woman to feel devalued and undesirable and undeserving of love as a woman. It also internally signifies to the woman that she is not worth being respected, honored, or worthy of a good man. Her self-esteem is pretty much done after emotional betrayals like this, and it takes much time to rebuild that. Now remember that I said almost every woman has experienced being lied to, cheated on, and betrayed by a loved one in a romantic relationship. So that would indicate that almost every woman has a damaged self-worth, self-esteem and personal value, which makes her unable to attract and sustain healthy loving relationships. Wow.

Having experienced such hurt creates future issues in our abilities to trust men in general. This inability to trust men prohibits us from connecting properly to a potential love mate, as we are unable to really be intimate with him due to our fears of being hurt again if we open ourselves up in that way.

Our inability to trust blocks our ability to connect intimately with people. Intimacy is the unique bond between two people that links them together emotionally, spiritually, and sexually. I submit that the purest form of intimacy occurs without sexual activity as intimacy does not require sexual activity, as most people would think.

The deepest connections that are made with a person are made through spiritual bonding; really getting to know the person and developing a true friendship through intense conversation and fellowship on a deep level. It is this type of connectedness that forms the basis of personal growth. It also provides the foundation for the glue that sustains marriages through challenges that are often brought on by stress, illness, work and other common problems.

Intimacy is the key-sustaining element in relationships that takes over when the intense passion of a being in a new relationship during the "honeymoon phase" expires. It is the enduring union based on common values, a true loving friendship and commitment.

Bonding intimately is difficult for those who have unhealed wounds from past relationships. This is so because in order for intimacy to develop and be sustained, a person must feel valued, cherished and respected as a person and by their partner. I stated earlier that the effects of unhealthy relationships are feelings of low self-worth, low personal value and a perception that others do not and should not respect us.

UNDERSTANDING HOW AFFAIRS HAPPEN

A specific reason is because intimate bonds are fractured and broken most often when a person transfers their emotional energy from their mate and the development of the relationship to other things or other people such as careers, children, outside interests and friends. While a strong relationships, built on a secure spiritual foundation, can weather temporary emotional absences, it is not likely to continue for long if the emotional absences go on indefinitely. Under these conditions, people may go out and connect or reconnect emotionally or spiritually with someone outside of their relationship with attempts to fulfill their needs for acceptance and understanding. Outside relationships such as these often begin benignly but may later evolve into becoming sexual. This pattern is most typical of "affairs of the heart" or affairs that pose the greatest threat to the primary relationship even more than those that are "just sexual."

So while sex may be the object of a partner's scorn, it is really the breakdown of communication and the ultimate severing of a bond that once existed that is really at stake. In essence, the betrayal that is attached to sexual infidelity may have already occurred long before on an emotional and spiritual level. Thus, while it may be one partner who strays outside the relationship, the responsibility for making it work remains the responsibility of both. While a person may claim that he or she was blind to anything in his or her partner's behavior that may have signaled a breach in intimacy, this in itself suggests that he or she is out of touch with the respective needs of the other.

The effects of affairs can be devastating and there are no quick or easy fixes to repair that type of damage. However, if both partners are motivated, then patience, honesty, and the skills of a professional can help the couple explore whether it is possible to reconstruct the once existed.

I want you to prevent affairs from occurring in your future marriage. To do this, you must get a good understanding about your past emotional baggage that would prevent you from trusting and connecting intimately with your mate; this is necessary before you enter into the relationship. Although we just touched the surface on the topic, you should have a thorough understanding of why affairs typically occur, the warning signals, and how to build a relationship built on true friendship and intimacy, which is a huge prevention strategy.

DO NOT DISMISS THE EFFECTS OF EMOTIONAL ABUSE

In addition to the effects of emotional abuse on a person I have discussed, I'll continue to bring special attention to the effects so that you may identify them in your life or the lives of others and receive healing. The effects are invisible to some degree as they live in the emotional and mental arena. These effects require a bit of extensive attention because out of your thoughts come your actions. This happens because you have suppressed or denied your emotions, feelings, and ideas to please the abuser for so long that knowing what you really feel, think or perceive as reality becomes unclear.

Your beliefs are affected. I'd like to call attention to one of the greatest effects that I feel emotional abuse inflicts on the abused, which is a distorted perspective on your thoughts, values and beliefs which are the core of who you are. This affects all other areas of your life when you go through life and are confused about what you really believe, your self-worth, your value and what you have to offer others. Your skewed understanding of your beliefs affects how you approach the world and the people in it.

You're more inclined to believe your partner than you are to believe yourself. You have, in essence, lost all sense of trusting yourself and your judgment. Have you ever reeled with a sense of hurt and injustice, or seethed with anger at the way you've been treated and then found yourself asking: "Is it reasonable or normal to feel like this? Am I misinterpreting what just happened to me? Maybe he was right. I am emotionally unstable or crazy."

Generally speaking, this could mean that you have become so brainwashed that you've stopped trusting in your own judgment about your feelings. Your mind keeps throwing up the observations and questions because deep down inside you know that what is happening is utterly wrong but you are just unable to feel the strength of your own convictions and take a stand for yourself and against being mistreated.

You are attracted to men who are emotionally unstable. The unstable man can be very loving but is often highly critical of you. He may tell you how much he loves you and in the next breath is uncaring or shows no consideration towards you. In fact, most often he treats you as if you were someone that he does not enjoy being around or that he truly dislikes. Another way to explain the previous statement is he treats you like he is doing you a favor by spending time with you or treats you as if you are "the enemy."

In these types of relationships, you constantly try to do everything you can to please him or make him happy but it never seems good enough. You're more like the pet dog or a doormat in the relationship than you are an equal partner. Your constant efforts to get his attention, quality time, or affection are usually met with limited success, as often he's dismissive towards you.

This leads the woman to wondering how her partner can treat her that way as some part of her feels that the behavior is undeserved and she in fact does deserve a loving partner. It is because she is trying to live in a love-based relationship when she is, in reality, living in a control-based relationship. Control-based relationships are based on a false sense of love, where deception and manipulation are used to control the abused. The mental abuser struggles with his feelings of worthlessness and insecurity, and uses his relationships to create for himself a feeling of personal power at his partner's expense.

You feel as if you are constantly walking on eggshells. There is a real degree of fear in the relationship most of the time. If it is not all out fear then it is anxiety about how your actions may or may not cause him to become upset or act out in some kind of way. You come to dread his outbursts, the hurtful things that he may find to say to you and the all-out drama that you will have to endure if he is confronted or unhappy about something that you do or say. Eventually you will no longer bring things to him or share thoughts that he may not agree with as to prevent the drama. No healthy relationship is motivated by fear or control.

Fear is not part of a loving relationship, but it is a vital part of a mentally abusive relationship and enables the abuser to maintain control over you, to be or feel how he wants.

The truth does hurt sometimes. In order to heal, you must be honest about who you are, where you are, how you got there and where you wish to go. If you are or have been in an abusive relationship then you must identify exactly what it was-abuse, and then you will be able to heal from the voids and brokenness that got you into that dysfunctional place.

You can heal. Mentally abusive relationships cause enormous emotional damage to the loving partner who tries, against all odds, to hold the relationship together and, ultimately, can't do it because her partner is working against her. How frustrating is that? Whether you are currently in a mentally abusive relationship, have left one recently, or years later are still struggling with the anxieties, low self-worth, and lack of confidence caused by emotional abuse, it is never too late address your need to heal and to begin that process.

Don't expect to change overnight. Typically, women who have suffered mental abuse expect radical change of themselves, but this is unreasonable. The abuse happened over a period of time and so does recovery from the effects, they will happen over a period of time. The effects of abuse are so profound on a person's identity and self-worth that expecting to heal right away is unrealistic. Be open to the healing process, which is a journey that continues all of your life as we are always growing.

Mental abuse recovery is a gradual process. The wounds of low self-worth and limited hope for a bright future literally block women from moving on and pursuing happiness. You must learn how to use the things that once blocked you to bless you. Use your pain to promote your purpose! What the enemy meant for harm, God will use for your good, praise God! You can overcome the effects of emotional abuse and keep yourself safe from it in the future by being honest with yourself about the decisions that you have made to subject yourself to abusive behavior. Face the facts about the emptiness or voids that you felt in order to put yourself in a situation that allowed another person to disrespect you, dishonor you and defile you. Those were your choices. By examining this process of why you made those choices, what made you remain there as long as you did, and how can you prevent yourself from getting into similar situations in the future will help you clear the clutter to get a new vision for your future relationships. Experiencing an abusive relationship in the past doesn't mean that you have to be in one again. You will be empowered as you create the life and the relationships you truly want as it really is within your power to do so.

CHAPTER 3: DATING GOD'S WAY

ATTRACTING KING CHARMING

If looking for love is tough, then finding King Charming will seem impossible, especially after a failed long-term relationship or divorce. The right perspective on dating and choosing ideal mates will increase your odds.

The first step in attracting a healthy, nurturing relationship is knowing what kind of partner that you want. It is best to do this while you are in your singleness and in a sound state of mind- healed- so that your standards aren't based on a specific person from your past or any unreal expectation of a person that you have created in your mind. Remember when we discussed writing the vision and making it plain? Well, this is exactly what you should do as it relates to being very clear about the internal and external characteristics and qualities that you desire in your mate.

DECIDE WHAT YOU WANT IN A MAN

While attractiveness may seem important right now, realize that looks fade with time. It is better to focus on quality of life characteristics such as having a deep spiritual grounding, being driven and motivated, or having a positive attitude and strong work ethic. Your list should include what is important to you, not to others. Write exactly what you feel is important and will make you happy.

In addition to making a list to create the vision for your ideal future mate, you should take a bit of time to look back at some of the men that you have previously been in relationships with to see how they measure up to your list for your ideal mate. Not that you plan to backtrack by dating someone in your past, but you want to see how far you were off at the time from having the mate that you really desired. This exercise will help you not to subconsciously compare people from your past to your new mate. Below are a few examples of important ingredients in sustaining a healthy relationship.

You need a man who is:

- God-focused, spirit-led and operating in purpose

- A provider who currently works to make money to support himself

- Honest, so you can trust what he says

- Loyal, dependable and ethical

- A friend who demonstrates his love for you

- Family-centered, an excellent father; is physically and emotionally present for his family

- Flexible, versatile and likes to relax and have fun

- Shares your vision on life but respects your opinions and ideas that aren't shared

- A giver, tither and shares easily with others

- Is romantic and affectionate

- Respects your freedom

- Comfortable around children

- Communicates well with others, especially you
- Secure with himself; extremely confident
- A leader; uses wisdom in decision-making and exercises good judgment
- Peacemaker; understands how to effectively resolve conflicts
- Understands submission and mutual respect in relationships

Use my ideal mate character list as an example to develop your own. I mentioned that you should spend some time evaluating the characteristics of your past mates to gain an understanding your dating pattern. This exercise will also help you to realize how far off your previous mates have been from the type of person that you truly desire in a Godly relationship.

Finally, this can give you an indication of your emotional state at that time of those relationships and an indication of how far you have grown or need to grow in terms of making wiser choices in dating. Now that you understand your errors, you will only engage in relationships with people who exhibit characteristics that you actually desire in a mate, as the goal is to marry one day.

So draft up a complete list of the names and the characteristics of old boyfriends, past lovers and ex-husband(s). Identify what attracted you to them in the first place. How many of their traits match your list of needs in relationships? If there is little correlation between what you needed and what you got, see how all the men in your life were similar. If, for example, the general qualities that you wrote for the mate that you desire were, "kind," "considerate," and "good-natured," yet your list denotes that you chose to date men who lacked those qualities, there is a huge internal conflict. Locate the cause of that conflict. Why did you choose to date men who lacked the personal characteristics that you needed from a mate? You must figure this out.

What factors influenced your decision to date mates who were not compatible? For example, were you attracted to their looks? Did they impress you with money? Or were you just lonely and fell into a trap to date because you were desperate. Be especially careful when you meet that "sexy" man that makes your heart race. If you are attracted to an extremely handsome man who is also bad-tempered, irresponsible, and abusive, then his attractiveness is not worth dealing with all of his negative characteristics.

You definitely don't want to invest yourself emotionally with this man. It's best that you just not to even allow yourself the temptation of playing around with him as not to set yourself up for getting emotionally attached when you already know that he does not meet the minimum qualifications for your ideal mate. Move on.

Don't settle for less than your expectations just to be in a relationship. Knowing what you want before you start looking for love helps separate the good from the not-so-good, and allows you to find someone truly compatible with you for a possible long-lasting love.

THE BASIC RIGHTS IN A RELATIONSHIP
Being in a dysfunctional or abusive relationship distorts your perception of what a healthy relationship looks like. I would like to

share with you what I created for myself when I began dating after my divorce so that I would have standards, healthy boundaries, and expectations for my future relationships. I call it THE BASIC RELATIONSHIP RIGHTS. These rights will be present in healthy relationships and marriages:

- » Your relationship with God and other positive people will be encouraged and supported.
- » Your opinions and feelings will be listened to attentively, valued, and respected.
- » Your core values, desires and needs will be prioritized.
- » You will not be charged with carrying undue weight of the relationship such as the financial responsibility of maintaining the home, *(This pertains specifically to the provision responsibilities of the husband in a marriage only).
- » You will be free to express yourself to the fullest in all areas of your life and be encouraged to grow as an individual in your own way.
- » You will be supported through tough times and helped in times of trouble by a reliable, dependable, and committed partner.
- » You will not have to take responsibility for your partner's deficiencies.
- » You will not be verbally, physically or emotionally abused.
- » You will be loved through your shortcomings and weaknesses.

» You will be shown love and affection without having to ask for it.

» You will see and feel love demonstrated towards you through daily actions not in just words.

» You will be free to pursue your passions, dreams, and achieve ultimate success in all areas of your life.

» You will be encouraged to be the best you possible by cultivating all of your spiritual gifts and natural talents without restraint.

» Your heart will be protected, nurtured, and secure from the threat of emotional danger.

DYSFUNCTIONAL RELATIONSHIPS EXAMINED

I'm sure that you have heard the expression that "good girls love bad boys?" Well, we have all seen the situation play out. A seemingly intelligent, successful, and beautiful woman gets involved with an all-around low-life and you look on and say, "Now why in the world did she get involved with him?"

The women in that type of relationship seems like they could get any man that she wants but she stays with this buster and puts up with his lying, cheating, not working, and even tolerates verbal abuse or physical abuse. We wonder why she doesn't respect herself enough to leave. Well, abusive relationships are very complicated, to say the least. Women often enter them because in some crazy way, they feel comfortable. For instance, some women interpret jealousy as "caring," or translate his thuggish ways as being confident or "manly." If he is really vigilant about where she is and whom she talks to, some women think that this must be an indication that "he really loves her."

The scary truth is, about one-third of American women have suffered some sort of childhood abuse – physical, sexual or emotional. Unfortunately, it likely came at the hand of someone they loved. So as adult women, they grow up to know this familiar world of warm fuzzies and cold prickles. This feels normal to them, and indeed, these are often the kind of relationships they seek out.

Usually, relationships do not start out emotionally abusive. However, all abusers have certain personality characteristics in common. Both women and men are drawn to mates with familiar personalities. This is why we often remark that so-and-so married someone just like their mother or father. This is because people raised in abusive families or who experienced or witnessed abuse early in life are attracted to people with the personality traits of abusers—people who seem familiar to them. Victims of abuse never understand why they are attracted to abusers or bad boys. There are many other specific reasons why the abused are drawn to abusers, just as surely as people from alcoholic families tend to marry potential drinkers.

The same happens to children who witnessed or experienced abuse at a young age. They usually go on to attract mates who are familiar to them as they attempt to replay scenes in our childhood: the hurt, pain and dysfunction with attempts to correct it, or "make it right" subconsciously in their adult relationships.

ADDICTIVE BEHAVIORS
Abusive relationships lead to low self-esteem and destructive

behaviors such as addiction. With addictive behaviors, an individual can become addicted, dependent, or compulsively obsessed with any activity, substance, object or behavior that gives him/her pleasure. Several researchers imply that there is a similarity between physical addiction to various chemicals such as alcohol and heroin, and psychological dependence involved in such activities as compulsive gambling, sex, work, exercise or eating disorders. Basically, the behaviors and activities may produce beta-endorphins in the brain, which makes the person feel "high." These and other medical research suggests that if a person continues to engage in the activity to achieve this feeling of well-being and euphoria, he or she may get into an addictive cycle. In so doing, he or she becomes physically addicted to his or her own brain chemicals, thus leading to continuation of the behavior even though it may have negative health or social consequences.

This may be a profound thought to some, but the pursuit of love can be addictive. It is a feeling that makes you feel high and on top of the world. When it is not in your life you can feel low, worthless and even lifeless. That is why we go through all kinds of things to potentially feel loved, even allow ourselves to be hurt in destructive and abusive relationships.

LOVE ADDICTS

I just drew a distinct similarity between being addicted to drugs or food and being addicted to the pursuit of love. People can be addicted to the pursuit of love instead of love itself because often those who are hurting themselves to find love in an addictive manner have not really encountered true love before- but a false love or their perception of love based on their past experiences. The person will compulsively date or sleep with people against their will to feel a sense of love.

Just like a drug addict, upon cessation of the activity, the sex withdrawal symptoms occur. There can be irritability, cravings, and restlessness when a person is not engaged in sexual behaviors with a man as that is what makes them feel loved, the closeness and perceived intimacy. Women have gone to great lengths to "get a man and keep a man" all at their expense. We must identify what voids are present inside us which makes us engage in unhealthy behaviors which we translate in our minds as love.

Are you a love addict? When you truly are full of real love, which is the love of God, you will not feel voided or pressed to fill emotional deficits with anything that resembles love to you. You will be secure, cautious and strategic in your pursuit of true love because you will understand your value. You also understand that everyone does not deserve your time and space and definitely not your love. This is freedom from the bondage of addictive behavior patterns and destructive relationships, which do not provide true love.

OTHER ADDICTIVE BEHAVIORS

The presence of addictive behaviors is a signal that your core or innermost being is not completely healed or full of God's love. In biblical terms, the substitution of another thing other than God to give you ultimate pleasure and fulfillment is also considered to be idol worship. You will spend time with those who you love, and it will not be just the "remaining time" after you have done everything else. This is a main cause of issues within marriages and leads to divorce.

Just as you should with your relationship with God while single, you should always give your partner the best part of you. They should never be made to feel like other people or things are more important than they are. They should not be a last thought to you, or perceive that you feel like it is a chore to spend time with them. Even when you become married, God still requires that we give Him the best part of us; you should practice this relationship principle while you are single so that when you become married, God is still the priority. He says in Matthew 6:33, "Seek ye first the Kingdom of God and all other things will be added unto you." Keep God first at all times, and He will reward you by adding the things that you desire to your life!

WHEN IDOLS OR ADDICTIONS TAKE THE PLACE OF FAMILY

Western culture promotes and rewards hard work. It is the basis of the Protestant work ethic that basically says that you should work hard, save your money, and anything in the world can be yours. Society implies that the harder you work, the more money you will have. The person who spends extra time at the office or studying (if it brings more money, job promotion, or better grades) is "being productive." In fact, many individuals who have spent most of their time working have made extremely positive contributions to society and have often changed history because of their hard work and dedication.

On the other hand, if the "work" or "ministry" becomes an

obsession to the extent that family, friends, other interests, or hobbies become unimportant and ignored, then the person is then thought to be a workaholic or work addict. Work becomes an idol then as all of the person's devotion is towards work or ministry to the exclusion of loved ones.

This directly leads to family problems and divorce and you should be aware of this prior to getting into a relationship. What generally happens is later, in old age, when the person realizes that all of his or her accomplishments really didn't mean as much as their family and they regretted having lost a lifetime of experiences and memories with their family.

Having a work-a-holic as a marriage mate can cause psychological problems in the children. For example, if a father promises his child that they will go to the basketball game on Saturday and never follows through for whatever reason (in this example, work) the child may lose faith in the father, especially if the behavior occurs frequently. Substitute work for studying, volunteering, or serving in ministry, and the effects of not being there for your children and family during impressionable times are the same. At the end of the day, after marriage the family should be a priority at all costs. Family is your first ministry before "church ministry" and we are to serve there with the greatest amount of commitment and dedication to yield the desired fruits of happiness, fulfillment and relational success.

How do destructive relationships turn into addictive relationships? If the relationship begins to be destructive, with constant mental or physical abuse by one or both partners, and neither person can break it off, then it is addictive. In our society, having family or friends to urge a couple to "keep trying to make it work" despite the presence of extremely destructive behaviors and abuse is common. However, when nothing has changed over a period of time, or the people involved do not express a desire to change by getting psychological help, deciding to strategically address the dysfunctional relationship before severe psychological or physical damage occurs would be better advice.

EFFECTS OF WITNESSING VIOLENCE IN OUR CHILDHOOD

In addition to many other things, children exposed to domestic violence learn the use of violence as a strategy to mediate their needs and wants. They see the violence between their parents and how in many cases the violence advances the preferred outcome of the aggressor.

The violence is viewed in many forms by the children and causes them to interpret love and relationships in a distorted manner. It may be through verbally abusive and demeaning language or physical gestures to intimate violence that send specific messages to a child about how they should express themselves or be treated based on varying situations.

There tends to be gender differences with regard to children exposed to domestic violence. Boys are generally at greater risk of learning that violence gets them what they want. Further, while relying on violence, there tends to be less reliance on verbal skills and hence these same boys are more at risk of inadequate communication or verbal relational skills such as dialogue and discussion to mediate their needs. Girls are at risk of learning that violence is normal and as a result can be more apt to accept violence within their relationships.

In terms of child and adult development children who have been exposed to violence can live out this past cycle in many different ways. Within the school settings, both boys and girls may be apt to use violence to get their way. Boys tend to use overt violent behavior such as bullying, intimidation and physical aggression whereas girls tend to use more covert behavior such as excluding others from their group and malicious gossip. Within adult life, men exposed to domestic violence in childhood are more apt to use violence in intimate relationships than other men who were not exposed to domestic violence in childhood. Similarly, women who as children were exposed to domestic violence are more apt to tolerate violence from intimate partners.

Generally, both men and women exposed to domestic violence in their childhoods may experience desensitization when it comes to recognizing domestic violence in adulthood. In other words, they may only recognize certain behavior as violent when it reaches a threshold near their childhood experience. This means that while they may resist or object to violent behavior as experienced in childhood, but they still manage to engage in or tolerate violent behavior not recognizing it as such, because it is less than what they experienced when they were young.

The issue here is that no amount of violence is acceptable and all violence carries consequences. So even if the adult domestic violence is less than experienced in childhood, intimate relationships will still be problematic and exposure to the children will as well.

Basically, if you were exposed to domestic violence as a child, consider discussing your experience with a trusted minister or a counselor who is knowledgeable in the healing process. In discussing your childhood experiences, it could also be helpful to explore current relationships and strategies for getting along and resolving differences when conflict arises. Nothing gets resolved that is not addressed; and you are only as sick as your darkest secrets. Exposing deep pain, negative emotions, or destructive behaviors are key to beginning the healing process.

REVISIT YOUR CHILDHOOD:
Application for the journey to inner healing.

Look back and evaluate your childhood to evaluate your experiences—begin to jot down memories that you have that stand out to you. Were you generally happy? Sad? Fearful? How did you grow up? Was your home environment secure? Did you see love demonstrated between your parents? Did you feel loved as a child? If not, why? Think about why you felt the way that you felt as this will help you to start to identify potential roots of negative emotions and dysfunctional thinking patterns.

THE DEVASTATION OF DIVORCE

Divorce, or the breakup of a long-term serious relationship, can be a devastating ordeal. The recovery from them both can be a difficult, extremely painful, and seemingly never-ending. Sometimes people don't recover at all. Others, although appearing to be past their divorce or breakup, still carry the pain with them, as well as the fear of getting close to another partner. With divorce specifically, it can be as painful as losing a loved one to death, but the grieving can be more lasting at times because the person is no longer a part of your life but still physically present in the world.

When you marry someone, the two people become one; they are one flesh, completely unified. You are becoming one, physically and emotionally, you both share one home, bed, family life, finances and the list goes on. You are most intimate with your spouse; they know all of your deep secrets, vulnerabilities and insecurities that others do not know about you. You tend to share the most memorable moments together such as daily mealtimes, couch snuggles, the birth of children, birthdays, anniversaries and other family events. Depending on the dynamics and complexities of the marriage, that can be a life altering and extremely traumatic experience that affects many people including children in the household, extended families and close friends.

If you have experienced a divorce, then you must take some personal time to be alone prior to dating or even thinking about re-marrying. I'd recommend at least a year, but it could take much longer, once again depending on the various factors necessary in your healing process.

Below are eight ways to help you to begin the recovery process, get your life back on track and prepare yourself for a bright relationship in the future.

1. Grieve deeply and completely. Many times people are terrified of dark feelings such as sadness, depression and anger. The intensity can make you feel like they'll take hold of your soul forever.

2. You must remember the old proverb that says, "This too shall pass," and you will get through it. Trust that although feelings of sadness and pain

are indeed strong, they won't last forever. Neither will they destroy you. As a matter of fact, you'll likely be a better person emotionally once you've let yourself work through the grieving process, begin to heal and learn to grow from it.

3. Grieve the future that you thought your marriage had. When people commit to each other for a lifetime many dreams and hopes are created for a life together. It is not simple to just let go of those hopes and dreams because we use dreams and hopes to guide us to our future. Consider what dreams and hopes that you had for your marriage and family. Then separately grieve each one. Know that your dreams and hopes are not dead as you are able to recreate them with someone else or even alone should you decide to.

4. Spend time talking with the supportive people in your life. When recovering from a divorce—or any devastating loss—it's critical for you to be allowed to speak your mind as often as you need to, but it should be with non-judgmental people who know how to listen to your feelings with complete love and acceptance. Many people aren't comfortable listening to others' dark emotions because they may be afraid of being overtaken by those emotions. This is why seemingly loving, caring people often try to "fix" us when we share our painful feelings and that is not always helpful. It's important that you're not interrupted or given advice like, "I told you this would happen" or "I

tried to warn you about him or her." No matter how true those statements may be, timing is everything and you don't need that type of support at that time.

5. Examine what happened in the relationship. In order for you to be able to come to terms with the divorce and to move on to create the wonderful life that you deserve, you need to understand what happened to cause it. This is the part of your journey where you'll have to be extremely honest with yourself. It'll do you no good to blame your ex, their family, the other woman, or yourself. You need to clearly understand the dynamics of the marriage between you and your partner and clearly trace the threads of the root causes that led to the divorce. You may find that the divorce had been pending for years as evidenced by many events and there was just a defining moment that ultimately provoked someone to take action.

6. Understand why you chose your former partner. This is critical in your healing process, as you will identify what relational needs or desires that you were attempting to fulfill and how you went about doing that by entering into that relationship or marriage. People choose relationships for many different reasons, the most popular being "in love." What many consider to be "in love" is often not really love at all-this feeling is usually lust or infatuation. Sometimes it is fear of loneliness, personal insecurities, and a desire to beat the maternal clock and have kids, the need for fi-

nancial security, or general pressure from friends and family to get married.

7. To grow past the effects of the failed marriage, you must learn to overcome perceived rejection that comes through the healing power of trusting in the love of Jesus Christ. His love for us is endless and unconditional while the love of others has limitations and many conditions. Once we learn how to believe in the reality that we always have access to true love through a relationship with Jesus we are empowered to overcome the rejection that we experience from people. You will begin to understand that no matter how others see you, treat you or feel about you, God's perception of you is most important. He really loves you and desires to be in a relationship with you despite your shortcomings and failures. If your heart has become stuck in feeling beat down by the rejection of people, rather than feeling uplifted by knowing God's acceptance of us, we need something to shock us out of captivity to other people's opinions and unfortunately that something is PAIN.

8. Appreciate the pain. In my opinion, pain is one of the things that God has placed in the world to let us know when we are off track or doing something wrong. Just like when our parents when we were young tell you not to touch a hot stove and we touch it anyway the pain of being burned causes us to not do it again, not necessarily our parent's instructions. I feel that it is the same with

painful life circumstances such as divorce. The greater the pain the less likely we are to take ourselves in that direction again. It's not that God is being mean to us, it is actually our own actions, our disobedience, and in most cases that causes us pain. Learn the life lessons and use the pain to push you into your God-ordained purpose.

We must come to accept that life isn't always fair and people are not always kind or trustworthy. They will hurt, betray, forsake and reject you, but your Father will never treat you that way. According to Ephesians 1:3-6, you have been forever accepted in the beloved of the Father. Rejection by others is only painful to experience if our hearts are secretly looking to other people to declare our worth to us instead of God's Word. If our hearts have become established in the knowledge of God's love for us, then we can handle the pain of rejection by anyone just as He did.

DEVELOPING AN INTIMATE FRIENDSHIP WITH GOD

Practice makes perfect and during your singleness is the time to learn how to be a good friend to yourself and others. You must learn how to cultivate an intimate relationship.

To have an intimate relationship with someone, you must know them in a very personal way. You must know who they are, their character, personality and behavior patterns, what they like, do not like, what makes them happy, and what grieves their heart. Knowing these things about your friend will help to you to love them by doing the things that make them happy and not doing the things that grieve them.

The Bible says that, "the fear of the Lord is the beginning of knowledge," Proverbs 1:7. The fear that is referenced is not spooky fear but actually can be translated as respect. Knowledge is power, but knowledge alone is nothing if you do not use it or act upon the knowledge that you acquire. Wisdom allows us to actually apply knowledge, not just "know things." Developing an intimate relationship with God requires that we know His heart or His feeling about life and relationships and how He operates within the two. We must use wisdom to respond to His feelings about life, love, and relationships just as we should in our relationships with our husbands. For example, a wise wife will always get God's perspective on every action before acting in her own will in making life decisions. If she has a Godly husband, their perspectives should not differ in spiritual things so she can never go wrong with adhering to this process.

This practice begins in our singleness through relationship with God as our husband. We learn to go to Him and seek guidance on things before just doing stuff as to not grieve Him in our actions and to get wise counsel. The same principle applies when you become married. Constant communication occurs between both parties to make sure that all are on the same page with life decisions, everyone's feelings are respected and no one is grieved.

You will see a continuing theme of respect and submission throughout later chapters of this book. as they are the main languages of love with your future husband other than expressing your love through friendships and your sexual relationship with him.

THE ENEMY'S WAR TACTICS IN MARRIAGES
One of Satan's tactics is to cause conflict and create discord within marriages. He uses disagreements that will cause people to create walls between each other in relationship. So with this in mind, you should always pursue peace despite personal feelings or disagreements to not allow walls to be constructed between you and your mate. Consistent communication and peace-seeking behaviors help to maintain a sense of unity in the home.

A WISE WIFE UNDERSTANDS TIMING
We must learn in our singleness that there is a time and place for everything. A foolish woman vents her emotions all of the time, but a wise wife talks to her husband respectfully at the right time. This does not mean that you just go along with everything that your husband says or does and do not voice your opinion about anything because he is the leader, but you use Godly wisdom to address him in the appropriate manner.

In the book of Ester, Chapter 1, Queen Vashti illustrated this point by being strategic in her approach to address important matters with her husband. She needed to discuss a very important business and ministry issue with her husband that dealt with his leadership and her desire to give him insight to change his mind about decisions that he would make.

She took a lot of time to fast, pray and seek God's timing in how she should approach her husband and even the words that she should say to him. She was not just concerned about being heard, getting her point across, or "making him do something." She understood that with God's direction on dealing with her husband, she could get more accomplished than she could on her own. Learn from Queen Vashti's example of using wisdom in communicating with your future spouse. This will also help you to build your friendship with him and trust God's leadership to guide you both effectively dealing with each other in your relationship.

HEALTHY RELATIONSHIPS BEGIN WITH HEALTHY FRIENDSHIPS

How do you develop healthy relationships and how do you operate effectively in them? I have found that there is generally little "real-life" training available in this area so people struggle with deciphering this information. So often, we connect ourselves closely with people who we really should not be sharing our space intimately as they do not qualify as true friends. Consequently, we fail at selecting "true friends" for our romantic partners because we never understood what qualities constitute a true friend.

I would submit that this is a fatal error that prevents us from experiencing love in its purest form because we choose to be in relationship with people who do not understand or possess love and unrealistically expect them to give us love. A person cannot give you something that they do not have.

As a result, we get accustomed to being in hurtful and dysfunctional friendships and experiencing a distorted form of love. My goal, in part, for writing this book is to shed light on these major relationship errors as to cause us to rethink the process of how to attract the right people into our lives, which is a basis for building healthy relationships and a precursor to sustaining a healthy marriage. Let's talk about true friendship and pure love.

GREAT MARRIAGES STARTS WITH GREAT FRIENDSHIPS

Some may not realize that the character traits of a good friend or best friend should be the traits that you desire in your ideal mate. The ultimate example of friendship is Jesus, who loved us, and sacrificed Himself for us despite how we felt about Him, even at the moment of His death. He sacrificed His life so that we might have life. Basically, he gave all of Himself for the benefit of people who could potentially never love Him back the way that He loved them. Despite feeling rejected, neglected, hurt and betrayed by those who He loved and even called friends, He didn't change His actions of love toward us—He wasn't moved out of love because of what others did to Him. That is a true love and real friendship.

CHARACTERISTICS OF A TRUE FRIEND

If your mate does not qualify as a true friend, then what is he to you? It is foolish to choose to be in a relationship or marry a person who doesn't qualify as a true friend. We will briefly summarize some basic qualities of a friend, considering also the characteristics of those with whom we should avoid associating. We have often called many people friends who in fact were not friends to us at all, so you must put people in their proper place in your life. Everyone is not meant to be "close." It is ok to love some people from afar and to have what I'll phrase a "hi and bye" relationship with them if they do not positively contribute to your life. Here are some characteristics of true friends to help you to identify people whom you should continue developing a relationship with:

- Are Faithful. Fairweather friends are numerous, but a true friend is a person who is there even when the going gets tough. They just don't show up when it is convenient for them or when they need something from you. They are consistently there for you when you need things too. You can count on them if you ran into a crisis to be supportive and help you as they are able.

- Will rebuke or correct us when necessary. They say things to you that may not be easy to say but need to be said to help you grow as a person. I am disappointed by the sentimentalism that pervades "friendships," some people flatter you when it is actually necessary to frankly correct you. A true friend is the one who is honest enough to tell us what we need to hear, rather than what you want to hear. Why is it, then, that some people feel that a wife should never correct her husband? Is it not better to be corrected by our closest friend than by an enemy? Sometimes the kindest thing a wife can do for her husband is to tell him when he has erred in judgment or that his idea or behavior is absolutely ridiculous—in a gracious way, of course.

- Thoughtful and tactful. A good friend is sensitive to our needs and speaks to us in such a way that we are encouraged and enriched from the conversation. It matters not only "what" we say, but "how," "when," and "why" we say things. Timing and tone of delivery of the message is very important as well. True friends remember things that are important to you, like birthdays, anniversaries, and special likes and dislikes. They are thoughtful by doing small things that may cheer you up when you are down or motivate you at the exact time that you need it.

- Sharpen us. Not only do we need to be criticized when necessary, but sometimes our thinking needs to be probed or stretched. A good friend does not allow us to become intellectually stagnant but prods us on to higher and greater thoughts. The Bible states, "Iron sharpens iron, so one man sharpens another." (Proverbs 27:17). The wisdom-filled book of Proverbs also says, "A plan in the heart of a man is like deep water, but a man of understanding draws it out." Isn't this true to life? Don't you seek to develop friendships with those who will challenge you to grow and expand your thinking? They will not want you to be mentally or intellectually dull but present you with new avenues of thought and encourage you to continue learning and exploring new things.

- Gives us wise counsel. Those whom we choose as friends should be marked by wisdom and the Godly counsel that they provide to us. Godly counsel is not given just by people of the cloth, but people who simply desire for us to be and have what God desires for us- a life of prosperity, wealth, health and good fortune. These people will give you spiritually based advice on how to get through difficulties, succeed, and be more Godly.

- Loves us just as we are. These people accept you for the person that you are even though you may not be fully aware of who that person is, they understand that you are flawed, still growing, and that you sometimes may disagree with them, not desire what they desire, and may not behave in a way that is pleasing to them. They will support you through difficult personal transitions and not judge you in your shortcomings by loving you through your challenges. They also do not try to make you become someone that you are not; they do not discourage your growth or excelling to greatness in any area of your life but they encourage it.

- Are honest. People who have demonstrated a consistent pattern of telling the truth, showing that their character is reliable, meaning that they do not change who they are based on circumstances, are the people that you want in your circle as friends in general.

CHARACTER WARNING SIGNS

As Single Wives, we must identify people who have qualities that would qualify them as friends and allow them more personal access to us as we see fit. We must also shun those who have characteristics that would disqualify them as friends and hinder our walk in wisdom and success. Now don't get me wrong, we should be kind to everyone, but that doesn't mean that we have to be in close fellowship with those who are not worthy of our personal space in being kind.

If we are not too closely associated with those who do not qualify as friends to protect our hearts, personal lives, businesses and ministries then we certainly should not marry them either, right?

Here are some character traits, which would seem to disqualify a person as a partner in marriage. Stay away from people who demonstrate the following character traits in general:

- **Fools.** It seems like a harsh term, but it's described in the Bible often in Proverbs. A fool is basically a person who hates instruction and fails to apply wisdom to their lives to grow and develop. One scripture states that, "He who walks with wise men will be wise, but the companion of fools will suffer harm"

(Proverbs 13:20). He should be wise in the dealings of his life with his time, money, business, and family interactions. He should demonstrate that he listens to and obeys Godly instruction. If he does not, then he is a fool.

- **Uncontrollable tempers.** If a man shows you that he is unable to manage his emotions by behaving inappropriately when upset, you should pay attention to that. How people deal with conflict or conducts themselves when things are not going their way is a true sign of their core character and maturity level. If a man yells, curses at you, or puts his hand on you at any time, then he is not ready for marriage or any other romantic relationship for that matter.

- **Evilness.** You are not going to like this, but evilness is not a deep as it sounds; it's evil to sin or to act contrary to the character of God. If a man lives a lifestyle of sin, not submitted to the will of God for his life, is violent, has trouble with the law, is consistently the source of conflict, unhappiness, or causes division with you or those close to you, then these are signals that he may be evil. Proverbs 24:1-2 supports this by saying, "Let us not be envious of evil men, nor desire to be with them; for their minds devise violence and their lips talk of trouble." This is clear.

- **Revolutionary.** There are some who are always out to change things such assoicety, government and other people. Desiring to improve things is not wrong, but the revolutionary is more bent on removing than improving. The revolutionary wants change for the sake of change, not change for the sake of improvement. Incidentally, some seem bent on finding a mate who needs improving—a sort of life-long project, meaning you!

- **Lacks self-control.** This means that he is unable to bring his body under submission or acts impulsively without using wisdom. For example, he has addictions to food, alcohol, gambling, drugs, sex or cannot keep himself from speaking out inappropriately. If he pressures you to have sex with him before marriage or does not try to be the leader by encouraging abstinence in the relationship, then you should pay attention to this as this is a sign of his inability to lead in Godly wisdom. If he has not gained control over his own body by being able to make wise decisions to abstain from sex, drugs or other addictions, then he will make similar decisions in other areas of your marriage. If he acts out irrationally by making poor decisions based on impulse or his selfish fleshly desires, then he will act out irresponsibly later with his body, money or your life in general.

- **Hypocritical.** He says one thing but does another or seems to live a double life. If his character is not consistent all the times or at least most of the time, then that is an indication that he has some identity issues and will be inconsistent in other areas as well. People who change their behavior depending on who they are around also make it difficult for you to know whom they really are- so it is impossible to develop a relationship based on truth.

- **Insecure.** We often think that women are the only ones who demonstrate insecurities in relationships but men do too. If a man lacks self-confidence, he will overcompensate in other areas like trying to control you, the relationship, or trying to deflate your confidence in yourself to make him feel better about himself. These are often the men who have to repeatedly tell you that "he is the man" in the relationship or that "he makes the rules and you need to just abide by them." These types of men are generally uncomfortable in the presence of other men, especially confident men. A true man—a leader—doesn't have to "make you follow him" by telling you to all the time, nor does he discourage you from having thoughts or opinions about him. Leaders, lead by example and teach others to follow them by demonstrating quiet confidence, good judgment in decision-making and acknowledging that he is not the only person with a brain—they understand that they can actually use their mate's help at times to make wise decisions. Insecure men generally do not make good leaders, as women who are intelligent, independent and successful threaten them. While confident men are proud to have such women on their team and are open to building success together as a team.

- **Instability.** Ideal mates should demonstrate a lifestyle of stability—in their key relationships, business, spirituality, and finances. A man who has moved around a whole lot professionally or personally tends to show a pattern of inconsistency in building a stable life or general inability to commit fully to any one thing. An ideal mate should show a reasonable history of being able to fully provide for himself without the assistance of others. That would mean maintaining consistent employment over a period of time in his life. You do not want to marry a man with poor work ethics, no drive or motivation to be successful in life, or no experience in being a responsible "head of household" meaning showing an ability to manage the affairs of his home. If he cannot take care of himself, his house and life matters, how will he be able to take care of you and a family?

TIPS ON INDENTIFYING GODLY LEADERS

Now that we have addressed identifying a few characteristics of underdeveloped men or those who are not prepared for the responsibilities of marriage, let's learn to identify men who are ideal marriage candidates—they are men who would qualify as true friends and Godly leaders.

If you have interest in God then church is a good place to become acquainted with men whom may have similar spiritual interests as you. You shouldn't join a church or religious group with the purpose of finding men. Although you are more likely to find a good man in church don't assume that just because he goes to church that he is Godly. Even if they are Godly, saved, sanctified and filled with the Holy Spirit does not mean that he is a good leader nor does it signify that you both are compatible in other areas of your life. Many women say that they just want a man who goes to church or is saved, but "saved" doesn't necessarily equal "suitable for you." There are tons of factors other than his relationship with God that need to be addressed before deciding if you and a man are good matches for each other for a lifetime partnership.

GODLY HUSBAND CHECKLIST

Earlier, I listed various characteristics of a true friend as well as a few character traits of men that would signal that you should avoid close relationships with them. The advice that I give to others in need comes from my life experiences in making poor choices in relationships, but also comes straight out of the wisdom from the book of Proverbs in the Bible.

At first glance in this book of wisdom, Proverbs seemed to say little to the woman who sought assistance discerning the qualities of Godly husbands, but I have come to see that this is not at all the case. In general, we can say that a woman should seek a man who qualifies as a true friend and is wise by applying Godly instruction to his life.

Here's a Godly husband checklist pulled from Proverbs to help you to further screen your potential mates in your dating phase:

- A wise husband is kind and compassionate
- A wise husband is honest
- A wise husband is hard-working
- A wise husband is truthful
- A wise husband exercises self-control
- A wise husband has a gentle tongue
- A wise husband is generous
- A wise husband is willing to be corrected (even by his wife) and listens to wise counsel
- A wise husband is a man of integrity
- A wise husband is faithful and reliable
- A wise husband is forgiving
- A wise husband is willing to admit he is wrong
- A wise husband is humble
- A wise husband is not contentious, but a peacemaker

- » A wise husband has control of his temper
- » A wise husband is a man who avoids excesses
- » A wise husband has a concern for others, especially the poor and the oppressed
- » A wise husband can keep a confidence
- » A wise husband fears God and is obedient to His Word
- » A wise husband is not a jealous man
- » A wise husband has a positive outlook on life

As I look at these characteristics of the wise, I am reminded of the qualifications laid down by the apostle Paul for elders and deacons in 1Timothy 3. I find a great similarity between the qualifications for church leaders and the characteristics of the wise in Proverbs. But should this come as a surprise?

After all, isn't Proverbs written to young men who will be leaders, instructing them to lead in wisdom? You want a man who qualifies in the areas of wisdom and leadership because this is the office that he must be fully capable to operate in as your future husband. He needs to qualify BEFORE the wedding, as these skills are not ones that you want to wait for him to learn along the way after you are married. Some he will, no doubt, but you need to see a general demonstration of his ability to operate in these areas sufficiently prior to him taking the leadership role as your husband. The consequences of your husband not operating in wisdom and leadership are severe and affect you, your children and your futures as a family so pay attention.

BIBICAL QUALIFICATIONS OF A GODLY LEADER
In this sense, 1 Timothy 3 only summarizes what Proverbs has taught in greater detail as he gives specific qualifications of deacons and overseers for the church, which from my perspective are the leaders, pastors, and ministry coverings of a Godly marriage, home over you and your children. That is serious, so you must be careful. Just as you are selective in choosing a pastor to lead you, cover you spiritually, and be directly participatory in you fulfilling your Godly purpose, the same process goes into selecting a husband as they, in essence, are responsible for the same duties in your life, if we rely on biblical instruction that is.

1 Tim 3-12: (I have added some emphasis but here is what the scripture says) [3]Whoever aspires to bean overseer (husband) desires a noble task. Now the overseer (husband) is to be above reproach, faithful to his wife, temperate, self-controlled, respectable, hospitable, able to teach, not given to drunkenness, not violent but gentle, not quarrelsome, not a lover of money. [4]He must manage his own family well and see that his children obey him, and he must do so in a manner worthy of full respect. [5]If anyone does not know how to manage his own family how can he take care of God's church (another ministry or business)? [6]He must not be a recent convert (new believer, or babe in Christ-immature Christian), or he may become conceited and fall under the same judgment as the devil. [7]He must also have a good reputation with outsiders, so that he will not fall into disgrace and into the devil's trap.

⁸In the same way, deacons (overseers, leaders, husbands) are to be worthy of respect, sincere, not indulging in much wine, and not pursuing dishonest gain. ⁹They must keep hold of the deep truths of the faith with a clear conscience. ¹⁰They must first be tested: (practiced living this type of lifestyle before getting into the office, in our case marriage) and then if there is nothing against them, let them serve as deacons (overseers, leaders, husbands).

¹¹In the same way, the women are to be worthy of respect not malicious talkers but temperate and trustworthy in everything. ¹²A deacon must be faithful to his wife and must manage his children and his household well.

CHECK HIS QUALIFICATIONS

From the nice framework that the Apostle Paul has laid out, he assist us in understanding exactly what to look for in a Godly husband. We should only date those who possess these qualities if marriage is our ultimate goal. This is not to say that the man must "perfectly exhibit" all of these qualities, as we stated earlier, no one is perfect and all of us will fall short from time to time, but his character should not conflict with this God-ordained standard for spiritual leaders as your future husband will operate in that role. You must think seriously about his ability to lead if you are interested in marrying a man that you would not be completely secure under his leadership, trusting his ability to operate in wisdom and make decisions naturally and spiritually for you and your children, then you may want to reconsider the idea of marrying him.

As an employer, I have made mistakes in giving people jobs for which they did not actually quality for, thus giving them more responsibility than they were capable of handling. In doing so, I had unrealistic expectations of the employee to be able to effectively carry out the job description of the position. This later caused much tension in the relationship because the job was not completed to standard, my expectations were not met, and the intended product was not produced. In the end, everyone was frustrated and the relationship usually didn't work out.

The scenario plays out the same way in relationships. We select men to date and marry that do not qualify for the job of husband. We have great expectations for them to excel in that role however they never possessed the necessary qualifications to effectively produce in that position, thus everyone involved becomes frustrated and the relationships generally do not work out.

For example, we date men who have no history of maintaining employment but we marry them and get upset when they do not want to work. We date men who lie, cheat and play games with us for years then marry them and get surprised when they are unfaithful. We date men who are immature and make poor decisions and marry them and are livid that they are not responsible and you now are forced into the position of mothering an "adult child". We date men who frivolously make children and do not take an active role of providing for or parenting them, then marry them and wonder why it seems like we are single parents.

Marrying a man will not miraculously change him into being the husband that you want him to be in your heart—those kinds of qualities are either present when you decide to marry or they are not. If they are not, then you are signing on to accept him just as he is. Please understand that people tend to become more comfortable after marriage so any presenting characteristics or behaviors are likely to intensify, times ten! Make sure that your man qualifies for the role assignment of a husband before you marry so that you both will not be disappointed and frustrated because your marriage expectations for each other were not met.

People have adopted faulty belief systems about how marriages should operate and about what the true designation of role assignments are within the marriage. These faulty belief systems about how husbands and wives should operate together in a family have been reinforced by poor marriage role-modeling in the media, our parents, other family members, friends and even Christian Leadership.

Without extensive studies in this area of healthy relationship building, dating can seem really scary and confusing especially to those of us who wish to obtain and sustain a long-lasting loving marriage one day. Often singles really do not know what the true role expectations are within a marriage and thus do not know what to do when married which is a recipe for disaster.

Marriage was meant to be an honorable, mutually beneficial and permanent institution. That's why in the Bible much emphasis was placed on the dating phase of marriage, which was a time period designated specifically to get to select and get to know a potential marriage partner. Now dating is used to have fun with someone and no more thought goes into it. The courtship period was so serious in the Bible that once commitments had been made, engagements, there was no easy way out of the relationship.

DATING GOD'S WAY

The scripture says, "Everything that was written before our time was written for our learning, so that we may through patience and comfort in the scriptures have hope" (Romans 15:4) This means that by using the life experiences of those in the Bible, we are able to learn valuable lessons about what things we should do, should not do, and have hope that we will obtain favorable results in our situations by applying this wisdom to our lives. In the Old Testament, people did great research on their potential mate's character, educational history, social reputation and families prior to making a commitment to date them let alone marry them. The qualifications to date a person were that they must show great potential to be an ideal marriage partner; they must demonstrate that they were capable of being a provider, leader, protector and "worthy" of the female's time investment in that type of relationship.

Basically, the man (or woman for that matter) had to prove to be an asset not a liability in terms of family and social connections—his reputation, financial capabilities and family lineage were all taken into consideration thoroughly before a woman would be approved to date him. Those folks understood the lifetime implications of choosing the wrong mate. As such, the entire family was involved in the dating process and often made the decisions for the daters because long-term vision and maturity were needed (which the daters may lacked) to have a mate properly.

One of the most pathetic marriages in the Old Testament is that of Abigail and her husband Nabal, described in 1 Samuel 25. She was wise and beautiful, while he was harsh and evil (1 Sam. 25:3). As his name indicated, he was a fool (Samuel 25:25).

I doubt that Abigail had much to say in the choice of this man as her husband since she was a woman of wisdom or maybe she was blinded by lust or moved by some other misguided emotion or family business arrangement. The long and short of the lesson of this story was that she had to go through much foolishness by marrying a fool and the situation was much easier to get into than to get out of.

DON'T MARRY A FOOL

For the one unfortunate enough to have married a fool, Proverbs offers no promises of an easy life or a quick fix for that situation. The assumption throughout the book is that a person must live with his or her mistake if it is in marriage. Divorce is never mentioned as the solution for a foolish decision concerning a mate. The picture painted of such a marriage is deliberately bleak.

One might think that the authors of Proverbs were somewhat cynical about marriage, having much more to say about its dangers than its delights. We must remember, however, that this book was written primarily to young men ("my son,") who had not yet married. One purpose of the Proverbs is to urge young men to consider their life's decisions carefully, since the consequences of a wrong choice are both painful and permanent. Choose wisely.

BUILDING A FIRM FOUNDATION: IMPORTANT CONNECTIONS

Marriage is the norm so far as Proverbs is concerned. The single life is nowhere presented as an alternative (such as Paul does in 1 Corinthians 7). Marriage is viewed as a divine institution, and it is God who gives a man a virtuous wife.

Godly men want women who are spiritually centered, family-focused, and confident within themselves. They do not seek to marry women who use their body to attract men. Know yourself. Be confident about who you are and what you have to offer in a relationship. Find out what you have in common and talk about your interests. Probe him about his thoughts about God, politics, culture, relationships and raising children. Learn each other's relationship expectations: What does he expect of his future wife? Her appearance? Household duties? Parenting styles? Sexual responsibilities? Get to really know him, his needs, desires and passions. Much time, prayer and discernment is necessary to effectively do this. The most successful relationships are not based on superficial things like looks but the deeper connections like spirituality and similar life visions and passions.

Ask him questions that help you to know him on a deeper level. See a few examples below:

- » What are his values? Life virtues? What is his vision for his life? What are his personal goals? Professional plans?

- » Is he financially capable of providing the standard of living that you desire? What are his financial goals? Does he manage money well?

- » How does he feel about children? If he has children, what is his plan for them being incorporated into the new marriage? How does he interact with the mother of his child(ren)? What is his parenting style?

- » What makes him upset, sad, happy, proud, scared or excited?

- » What kind of relationship does he have with his mother? Sisters(s)? Father?
- » Has he been married before? If so, what lessons did he learn from that relationship?
- » What qualities does his ideal mate possess? What attracted him to you? What are his primary needs within a relationship?
- » Where does he see himself in 1-3-5-10 years?
- » What things can he live without? What this can he not live without?
- » What are five things that he feels are most important to his life?
- » If there were no limitations of his life, what would he do? Where would he go? What things would he like to have?
- » What has been his greatest accomplishment(s)? Failures? Joys? Fears?

These types of questions give you a good start to begin quality conversations that should allow you to get to know who he really is and if the two of you have enough in common to maintain a good friendship and make a successful life together...After all, what his zodiac sign and favorite color is will not matter when you two have completely different views on the things that are really most important in life.

Build a strong foundation by just focusing on your friendship and not marriage right away. Remember, you also want to get to really know him before you consider starting a serious relationship. If you notice something you don't like about him or feel would be an issue in a potential "serious relationship," you can remain his friend and no one loses anything.

Godly men look for women who are responsible, moral, and eventually ready to settle down. They don't date women who just want to fool around with them. Make sure you are ready to start a committed relationship; that means that you are physically, mentally and emotionally available to commit your life to serving another person as their "help-meet" in marriage.

SELF-EVALUATION: ARE YOU DESPERATE TO DATE?

Women are emotional creatures and are very sensitive, but in dating that's a different story because women need to really take to heart the things they do. Sometimes the emotional decisions that we make during the dating process can actually prevent us from attracting and keeping ideal mates. Presenting dating desperation can cause men to become distant and aloof and will result in them not returning phone calls, emails or even visiting. I won't say that no man wants a desperate woman because some men actually seek out desperate women, but those are not the types of men that you really want.

Women need to pay close attention to their behavior because you do not want to come off as being needy, clingy or desperate in general. That type of behavior would turn off ideal mates. I understand that as women, we have a desire to be loved and cared for, yet there are some things that we kind of forget when it comes to expressing that. We need to understand what kind of behavior will keep or scare men away.

Let's shed some light on how we may send signals that we are desperate for a date or relationship as we never should be in that position. You date when you "want to" not because you feel that you "need to." If you feel that you need to date someone, then you probably should wait a minute to date until it is less urgent to you.

You are still in the "women in development" stage and have not yet graduated to the mental, physical, and emotional maturity level of single wives if you are:

» **A serial dater**—This is one of the ways a guy can tell if a woman is desperate for a date. She's constantly with a guy and usually ones that don't stick around very long – she can't be alone for long. She's in and out of relationships before they really get started. Guys can tell if a woman is needy and clingy because she's changing boyfriends like clothing and always has to have one.

» **Planning your entire life and existence around a man**—This is something that would drive the average man nuts because she plans everything based on him. She also expects her man to rearrange his schedule to make sure that she's penciled in 90% of the time. She will begin planning her future prematurely by already thinking marriage and kids before the second month of dating! This behavior signals that the woman is not mentally or emotionally stable. Men like to take their time in dating and getting to know a woman, but usually after the first few months to a year, men know if the woman is the person that they plan to marry. Ladies, if you want to keep a guy around longer than a month, refrain from the chatter about marriage and babies, until the time is appropriate to address those subjects.

- **Having attachment issues**—This can creep guys out when ladies start getting attached to them too fast, such as wanting to be around them all of the time and even more saying "I love you" after only a few dates. This can border on excessive, and many guys will dip out when this happens by not returning phone calls.

- **An excessive communicator**—You have the need to call, text and tweet, IM or email him way too much. The fact is that we all like to have that sense of communication with those whom we are interested in or involved with. Some women just take it overboard by calling, texting, or emailing a guy more than several times a day. What women don't realize is that guys find it annoying when they're having their phone blown up with calls and text messages or excessive emails. It's fine to text occasionally if the guy's someplace where he can't answer the phone, but to text or call every few moments is excessive and you are sure to get the voicemail and blocked soon.

- **Are an excessive online dater**—If you have a profile listed with every online dating site, then this could be an indication that you may be a bit desperate. That's just too much.

- **A pushover**—These types of women are ones that make many guys want to dip out quickly and not look back because the women are void of a personality and identity. True men appreciate women who have individual thoughts, feelings and opinions and are not afraid to challenge them on things. Some guys prey on women who basically have no outstanding qualities because it is easy for them to mold and manipulate her into being whoever he wants her to be.

» **An annoying friend**—If you always want to spend time with your man then you need to get a life and finds some things that you like to do on your own. Every now and then men want you to spend time doing other things or being with other people. When a woman wants to be around her man all the time it can become annoying and after a while, some independence is good. Do your own thing sometimes.

» **Too sentimental**—This is a classic sign of emotional weakness because the mushy, romantic sentiment can lose meaning after a certain point. If you are always crying and whining about something or complaining about how hurt you are, it can be a bit much to handle and guys will likely pull away.

» **Always reminiscing, talking about a past partner or spouse**—We're all curious about our potential mate's previous life with someone else and talk about this in the beginning of relationships, but when it gets to the point where it becomes the normal part of conversation it can take its toll on a relationship. Guys especially feel out of place when they're dealing with a woman who's constantly talking about past boyfriends and husbands since it makes them feel like they're still in the picture.

» **Too ready to meet his family**—There's that rule of thumb in dating that you should give a certain amount of time before introducing your mate to your family and friends. Do not be pushy in this area – just let it come up organically.

» **A territory hog**—This is a sign of insecurity when a woman has to constantly cling on to a guy when other females are in his presence and she always has this look like she's ready to fight if someone seems to be looking at her man. What women don't get is that men like women who are secure with themselves and not acting like they're in "combat-mode" all of the time. Even if other women try to pull slick moves on your man, just play it cool and relax...see how he handles the situation.

» **A video chick dressing in attire that's too provocative or inappropriate**—This is also an indicator of insecurity and low self-esteem when a woman has to show off her body in an attempt to be sexy. Single wives are classy. You can be sexy without showing all of yourself to everyone. That type of attire should be reserved for you and your husband in your private quarters—then you can be whoever you want to be!

» **An agreer**—Always agrees with what a guy says. This also points out that you may not be able to think for yourself. Have a mind of your own; voice your opinions respectfully and stand on what you believe at all costs.

SINGLE WIVES DATING BOUNDARIES

In addition to the basic boundaries that I listed in previous chapters that should be present in any healthy relationship, single wives have a bit of a higher standard for relationships as we represent Godliness and must demonstrate virtue and honorable character. You must be able to set appropriate boundaries for your dating relationships and state them at the beginning of your courtship so that you both are responsible for maintaining them.

At the end of the day, you are the guarder of your temple, so no one can force you to be in a situation that you do not want to be in. Avoid undue temptation. Although the man should respect and maintain Godly guidelines for your interactions, you both should find ways to avoid sexual interaction if the desire is too strong. The first boundary is no sex before marriage period. People have come to define sex so many different ways, but sex is sex and you should cherish yourself enough to preserve such a gift to present only to your husband. This includes abstaining from physical intercourse, mental imaging, phone sex, oral sex, body rubbing, naked massages, "dry humping" and sexting. I think that I've covered it.

Surround yourselves with Godly friends who hold the same values and will assist you in upholding your commitment to God. Godly friends with similar values will hold you accountable to living holy. Also, literally having extra company with you on outings distracts you from sexual thoughts or tempting opportunities to act on normal sexual desires.

It is normal to feel sexual attraction to your mate, so you should set time limits for dating interaction and make sure that you all choose not to go places that are enticing...like your bedroom!

This means that you should enjoy each other's company during reasonable hours of the day. There should be no overnight outings or "sleep-overs" under any circumstances.

A respectable man should leave your home at a respectable hour; -he should not be making excuses as to why he needs to spend the night, no matter how much you both feel that you can "handle it." Our spirit is willing (to do the right thing) but our flesh is weak (Matthew 26:40), that means that although we may have good intentions not to engage in sexual activity, our bodies can have other plans when we get close to a good looking, good smelling, romantic man who we desire to be with! Now, depending on how long you have been dating you both will decide the terms of your interaction and acceptable locations to help you prevent "mishaps."

No matter how long you have been dating, too much snuggling, rubbing and kissing can cause problems. Find ways to show each other affection in non-sexually stimulating ways. That can be difficult when you are really "feeling someone," but God will give you both assistance if you desire assistance. He says in 1 Corinthians 10:13 that, "with every temptation God will always give you a way of escape so that you will be able to bear it and not give into the temptation —if we desire not to" (emphasis added).

SELF-CONTROL AND PERSONAL RESTRIANT WITH SEXUAL URGES

Dating Godly men requires patience and self-control. Sex outside of marriage, or fornication, is unacceptable. Show intimacy by holding hands, hugging, or telling him how you feel about him. However, as difficult as it may be, avoid kissing.

Singleness is the time to practice our voluntary self-service of sacrifice with our flesh in commitment (marriage/honor) to God so that the concept will not be new once we get married. That's why celibacy is so important. Celibates use abstinence and religious hermits use isolation to grow in our service, obedience, character, holiness and love of God, so we use marriage for the same purpose. Practice makes perfect!

BE INTIMATE WIHTOUT BEING SEXUAL

I mentioned earlier that intimacy is a deep profound connection built between two people that often has very little to do with sexual interaction. It is created by really getting to know a person on a spiritual level—their inner person and building trust. You cannot learn to trust someone if they do not have opportunity to be trusted with things that you value, your temple or body, or personal information that you would only share with true friends.

Often times we talk to our girlfriends about our fears, weaknesses, and deficiencies and never share this information with our mates. Typically, the best way to deal with doubts and insecurities is to talk to your romantic partner about them. When people are suspicious or uncertain, they often try to hide their true feelings from their partners, but ignoring one's emotions never works. Our feelings always get the best of us and influence our behavior whether we like it or not.

So when people have doubts, if they do not talk about it, it comes out by way of sudden mood changes, acting overly controlling, being too sensitive, clingy or needy, and causing unnecessary arguments.

Ironically, one's insecurities can even lead a person to flirt with others as a way of getting a partner's attention or showing him what it feels like to be insecure. Again, a lot of research shows that talking to a partner about feelings of insecurity is the best way of dealing with it. As a general rule, when talking about such issues, it helps to focus on one's feelings and not necessarily a partner's behavior. Basically, do not blame or attack a partner because you feel insecure; rather, explain how you feel to them. Use statements like "sometimes my doubts get the best of me and I don't like feeling this way but..."

If you can talk directly to your partner about how you feel, you are less likely to act in ways that create more distance and disruption in your relationship.

In fact, people often feel closer when they can talk to their partners about their deep-rooted problems in a constructive manner. Talking about problems is very important when trying to overcome one's insecurities while building a genuine friendship and with hopes of moving forward into a deeper level of friendship or marriage.

REBUILDING SELF-ESTEEM

A person's self-esteem usually takes a beating during the divorce process or a bad break-up. To help rebuild your self-confidence, you need to focus on your attitude. Attitude is simply a state of mind. By focusing on the positives in your life, you can begin to feel better about yourself and life in general. The following tips will help you to rebuild your self-esteem:

» **Affirming what's good** — When your self-esteem is in the dumps, it's easy to beat yourself up and think of yourself as a failure. Replace all those self-defeating thoughts with affirmations of the person you want to be. List the things that you are good at, recount your past successes, and remember the good things that people have said about you that makes your self-esteem soar. Use words like, "I am happy, strong, smart, resilient, ambitious, beautiful, etc..." or whatever image that you would like to see yourself as. Review this list often to build your self-image. Remember... "As you think in your heart (about yourself) so shall you be," (Proverbs 23:7 emphasis added).

» **Thinking positively** — Along these same lines, replace your negative inner dialog (the conversations with yourself about why you cannot do something) such as "I can't do it" or "I'm just no good" with self-esteem building statements like "I can do all things through Christ who strengthens me! (Philippians 4:13)," "I am successful," or "I have what it takes." It may feel funny at first, but if you say these affirmations every morning to yourself, your mind will start to focus on them and start believing them to be true even if you don't when you begin saying them.

» **Letting go of the past** — Put past mistakes into perspective. You can't change the outcome, so try to see it as a learning experience. Make any amends that you need to, and then vow to hanvdle things differently in the future. Realize that everyone makes mistakes and let it go. Choose to focus on what is positive in your life.

- **Letting go of perfection** — By thinking that you need to do everything perfectly, your confidence ends up taking a beating. You end up with a list of imagined "should" and "musts" to meet your vision of perfection. Instead, decide what things are fine just the way they are, and quit worrying about them. Whatever you decide to change should be because you "want to" or "choose to." By allowing yourself to not be perfect, your self-confidence grows as you accept the true you.

- **Making changes** — If there is something that you would like to change, stop procrastinating, and do something about it. Worrying and rehashing your troubles all the time just brings you down. Decide what needs to change, and break it down into small chunks. By having daily manageable goals that you can accomplish you will find a sense of purpose, a continuous feeling of success, and improved self-confidence. You can see yourself moving in a positive direction and won't be overwhelmed.

- **Interacting with others** — Spending quality time with positive people is a good idea. They can boost your mood and give you a different perspective on your situation. True friends always see the best side of you. When they give you a compliment, believe them. In return, don't be afraid to compliment or do something nice for someone else. Doing for others can boost your self-esteem by focusing outside yourself and knowing that you brought happiness to someone else.

Most of all, realize that you have choices in life. You can choose to be content with what you have now, or you can change. Your inner peace, self-image and confidence in who you are determines your success, not what others think about you.

CHAPTER 4: GOD'S PLAN FOR MARRIAGE

HOW IMPORTANT IS THE WEDDING?

The Bible does not give specific details or directions about a marriage ceremony, yet it does mention weddings in several places. Jesus attended a wedding in John 2. Wedding ceremonies were a well-established tradition in Jewish history and in biblical times. Scripture is clear about marriage being a holy and divinely established covenant. It is equally clear about our obligation to honor and obey the laws of our earthly governments, which are also divinely established authorities. But, before we go any further, let's stop and examine the issue. There are three commonly held beliefs about what constitutes a marriage in the eyes of God:

- » The couple is married in the eyes of God when the physical union is consummated through sexual intercourse.

- » The couple is married in the eyes of God when the couple is legally married.

- » The couple is married in the eyes of God after they have participated in a formal religious wedding ceremony.

Let's break this down and see what the Bible says about the marriage covenant.

In Malachi 2:14, we see that marriage is a holy covenant before God. In the Jewish custom, God's people signed a written agreement at the time of the marriage to seal the covenant. The marriage ceremony, therefore, is meant to be a public demonstration of a couple's commitment to a covenant relationship. It's not the "ceremony" that's important in a marriage though, it's the couple's covenant commitment before God.

THE WEDDING CONTRACT

Let's carefully examine the traditional Jewish wedding ceremony and the "Ketubah" or marriage contract, which is read in the original Aramaic language. In the marriage contract, the husband accepts certain marital responsibilities and provisions for his wife. He agrees to provide food, shelter, clothes and promises to care for the emotional needs of his bride.

Only if we could utilize this contract model as the contractual basis for marriages in Western culture, as it would alleviate so much confusion about the basic roles and responsibilities of the husband and wife. It would be very simple, just go by the contract and add other items that are important to each of you after the basics are covered, like who provides for the family or who cares for the children.

The marriage ceremony was not complete until the contract was signed by the groom and presented to the bride. This demonstrates that both husband and wife see marriage as more than just a physical and emotional union, but also as a moral and legal commitment. The Ketubah is also signed by two witnesses, and considered a legally binding agreement. It is forbidden for Jewish couples to live together without this document. For Jews, the marriage covenant symbolically represents the covenant between God and his people, Israel.

For Christians, marriage goes beyond the earthly covenant also, as a divine picture of the relationship between Christ and his Bride, the Church. It is a spiritual representation of our relationship with God. If we actually looked at how we relate to our mates as how we are exemplifying our relationship to God, it should cause us to take action and make immediate changes in our behavior and love shown towards our partners. In marriage, you should daily ask yourself, could others use the way that I love my mate to understand how God loves us? Well, that is what happens whether you know it or not, people are watching you, so keep that in mind when interacting with your mate!

AREN'T WE MARRIED IN GOD'S EYES IF WE LIVE TOGETHER?

When Jesus spoke to the Samaritan woman at the well in John 4, he revealed something very important, something we often miss in this passage. In verses 17-18, Jesus said to the woman, "You have correctly said, 'I have no husband;' for you have had five husbands, and the one whom you now have is not your husband; this you have said truly."

The woman had been hiding the fact that the man she was living with was not her husband. According to the New Bible Commentary notes on this passage of Scripture, Common Law Marriage had no religious support in the Jewish faith. Living with a person in sexual union did not constitute a "husband and wife" relationship. Jesus made that plain here. You are basically giving free benefits and privileges to a man without him making commitments to you and accepting the necessary responsibilities of caring for you when you have premarital sex with a mate.

WHY DO MARRAIGES FAIL SO OFTEN?

The general statistics holds steady that approximately one out of two marriages fail. So that means that half of nuptials end up in divorce court. Today, it is commonplace to hear that if a marriage isn't going as expected then you can throw in the towel and just get you a new marriage. Commitment, dedication and the hard work that it takes to make a marriage function successfully seem not to be advised any longer.

There are general reasons that marriages do not work out and I've mentioned some of those reasons in my personal testimony at the beginning of this book. One of the main causes of failed marriages are broken people entering into marriages that they are emotionally, physically or mentally incapable of maintaining successfully.

Combine this with the fact that people generally have unreal expectations of their mates, misunderstanding what marriage is really about and are literally unprepared for taking on their marriage role. That combination is a recipe for disaster!

For example, if based on the incomes of an engaged couple it would take two people to work to financially carry the household responsibilities then it would be unrealistic for one person to expect that once married, they will not have to work. This will cause a problem, and troubled finances are one of the leading reasons that people divorce.

In another example, if it has been discussed that one partner is clear about having children and the other partner does not wish to have children at all, it is unrealistic to believe that either person will change their mind after the wedding. The reality is that the wedding doesn't change people's core beliefs or character traits.

The problem is that most singles never have difficult conversations about tough issues like financial planning, childbearing, parenting and marital role expectations prior to their weddings.

Communication is key; once you discuss an issue, receive an answer on a topic, you should accept it as truth and not expect that the person's viewpoint will change-ever. Now if their viewpoint happens to change in the future then you will be pleasantly surprised but you should not expect it to change, so then you will not be disappointed if it doesn't. Topics that should be discussed in detail to gage a full understanding of each person's perspective and vision for their ideal marriage are:

- » **INTIMACY**—How does each person view it? Express it? How much is needed for each person? Does either person have intimacy issues? If so, these things should be addressed prior to marrying through couples counseling, as intimacy is a huge core part of sustaining a marriage.

- » **KNOW THYSELF**—Individuals in relationships tend to latch on to whoever they're with and become co-dependent instead of discovering their own worth and embracing their singlehood before getting into a relationship. A partner should enhance who you are as a person not replace who you are as a person. Many people distort this principle. All couples should have a bevy of things that they like to do together, or places they enjoy going, but they should have individual interests as well, so, they don't smother each other and extinguish the fire. What are your core values? Beliefs? Life virtues that shape your actions? These core beliefs and values should not be changed in a relationship but enhanced and further developed with the support of a loving partner who accepts and validates you for who you are and who you will be.

- » **UNHEALED HEARTS**—Sometimes people jump into relationships without healing from past hurts and have open wounds. Basically, they have unresolved emotional issues. These unresolved issues are normally with someone from their past, an ex-husband, ex-boyfriend or parents and a partner can idealize the ex or harbor anger or resentment towards them and hold the new mate to an unfair expectation of being like a significant person in their lives who previously hurt them. Conversely, by comparing a new partner to an old one, a person could even be held to a standard that they can never meet in areas of displays of affection; sexual gratification or material provisions. The wise thing to do is to fully resolve your past feelings about previous relationships and then you will be free to wipe the slate completely clean with new expectations developed with your new partner that aren't influenced by your past.

- » **INAPPROPRIATE BEHAVIOR**—Many people in relationships may knowingly or unknowingly display improper behavior with someone who is in a relationship or allow people they know are in a relationship to relate inappropriately to them. Whether it's using terms of endearment, even playfully, with someone you're "not" in a relationship with, the rule is, if you want to keep your relationship intact, draw boundaries and don't allow anybody to cross the line no matter how friendly you've become with them. If you introduce behavior like that in someone else's relationship, then you are opening the door to it in your own relationship. Many relationships have fallen apart over much less.

- » **JEALOUSY AND INSECURITY**—These two things ruin thousands upon thousands of relationships every year. This is where getting in touch with yourself before coupling into a relationship should be mandatory. You should be whole and appreciative of yourself and know your self-worth before you come into a relationship. It shouldn't fall on your partner to boost your self-esteem and stroke your ego. It's unfair and can become a nuisance. But on the flipside, if the jealousy and insecurity is warranted because his or her co-worker or friend is disrespecting your relationship, you have a right to feel what you feel and their job is to handle it so you no longer feel that way. Get a grip on jealousy, but learn to also put friends in their place even if it hurts their feelings, and that will let your love thrive, flourish, and grow.

» **TIMING**—When is the ideal time for marriage? How long should an engagement last? When will each person be "ready" to get married and what are the factors that determine that in each person's life. No one should ever feel pressured to get married quickly and no one should be made to wait an extensively long amount of time for the other person to get ready. An ideal engagement plan would: outline how long the engagement will last, what individual and team items will be accomplished during the pre-marriage phase and how will outcomes be achieved, monitored, and documented. I know that it seems a bit business-oriented but marriage is a contractual arrangement glued together with love. You must have clear expectations of what each participant desires and expects throughout the relationship to prevent surprises after the wedding and either party feeling trapped in a situation that they did not sign up for.

» **COMMUNCIATION STYLES**—Communication, communication, and communication. There can never be too much communication in a relationship. If either person has trouble communicating their feelings in a socially acceptable manner then developing communication skills should be worked on during the engagement, as this skill is required to sustain a healthy marriage. Both partners should be well versed in verbal and non-verbal communication and also the manner in which your partner expresses themselves at different times. You must know their "love language" to effectively speak to each other without sending unintentional error messages to each other. I suggest that extensive time be spent on understanding communication so, I recommend you guys reading, *The Five Love Languages of Love*, as a great pre-marriage guide on effective communication.

» **TRUST**—What has been each person's experience in previous relationships with trusting others and how has their trust expectations been met or unmet? Trust must be discussed extensively to better understand what the other person needs to feel that they are in a secure relationship and their trust is not violated. We all have had our own personal experiences where our trust has been tested and violated by others and boundaries must be set in this area with all relationships so that no one is unknowingly hurt. If a person is experiencing difficulty with trusting people, then this must be dealt with through consistent counseling- individually and as a couple. If there is no trust between partners, then there is not a relationship. Both parties must feel secure in allowing the other person to hold their heart and care for it. That takes trust.

» **SELFISHNESS**—This may be difficult to accept, but we are all self-centered, we tend to dismiss other's feelings at times and may say hurtful things during mood changes. To look outward is to be concerned about the feelings of others. You can ask yourself, "Did I make him happy today or did I hurt his feelings?" Most of the time because of pride we tend to hurt others because we are most concerned about our own feelings. In order to maintain unity in a relationship, we need to remove our pride. How? By thinking and caring more for the other person and trying to serve him better.

- » **AFFECTION**—Does your mate show PDA (public displays of affection)? Do you love to be touched, hugged, and cuddled often? If so, then your mate needs to know that early and you need to know what kind of affection your mate desires as well. We are social people. We interact with each other differently. One of the best ways to relay our feelings and concerns is through gentle touch, a warm hug, a peck on the cheek, and other subtle but powerful means of showing our affection. It is important to say, "You know that I love you..." to the person dearest to you. However, you need to also show your love outwardly one way or another. For example, when you marry, you should make it a point to kiss or hug your husband every time that you leave each other. Affection brings warmth and closeness to each other and both people should be comfortable showing the other mate affection in the way that they desire it.

- » **NOT GOD-CENTERED**— "Put God first in your Life." Christians believe that GOD is LOVE and experience His immense love. With the awareness of putting God in the relationship, we elevate that relationship into a higher plane, a higher level. This is an INCREDIBLE way of enhancing the relationship. Trust, concern, caring, being kind, forgiveness, etc., naturally follows with this awareness that God is around, guiding the relationship. Putting God first is more than something that you say when you talk to people— "We put God first." Rather, this is demonstrated by your lifestyles as singles and how you make decisions that are according to God's Word. If you both are not submitted to the will of God and are not obedient to Him in all areas of your lives then your life is not God-centered and He is not first in your life. Practice this while you are single and no person should be able to make you compromise your core relationship with God. This creates the foundational stability for your future marriage and weaves the 3-strand chord that is not easily broken-God, the husband and the wife.

» **ABSENCE OF FRIENDSHIP**—"We're lovers, not friends" as a saying goes. But let's face it, being married for say seven years would make any couple fall from the "romantic" state and settle to a "dry" relationship if a genuine friendship is not present. Keep in mind that if you were friends before you got married, remaining friends will be easy. True friends genuinely care about the other person's well-being and happiness, desire to stay unified, and are willing to invest whatever is necessary for the betterment of the relationship so this should never change. Given that you have great communication, then all you have to do is press the "refresh" button and consciously re-new your friendship instead of trying to develop a friendship from scratch years into the marriage when you experience time periods where you start not to like your mate. This happens because you didn't take the time to get to know your mate before marrying your mate and later realize that you actually do not have much in common. Your marriage mate should be your BEST FRIEND! Other people should supplement this core friendship and not replace it in any way.

DIVORCE-PROOF YOUR MARRIAGE

It is a terrible feeling to wake up one day after being married for any period of time and realize you don't have anything in common with your mate and you both are growing a part. Love, while it can be energetic and romantic in the very beginning, during the "honeymoon phase" it still has to be fed with commonalities for it to grow and thrive. You need to have more than just a thing or two in common to forge ahead and make a relationship last.

Many people discard the need to have things in common and then they soon realize that after they're together for ten years that they don't even like the same kinds of foods or television shows. This can disrupt lives. Small things foster togetherness. Learn where your partner would like to one day travel, what their idea of relaxation truly is as well as what kind of books you both like to read. Your common trends are the framework of your relationship in the future after the honeymoon is over.

GOD'S ORIGINAL DESIGN: MARRIAGE 101

It is such a faulty assumption that one can jump into a marriage and "just do it" without having an accurate understanding of the institution based on God's perspective. God is the original designer of the marriage model; thus it would behoove us to obtain its purpose, operational functions, and role assignments for the involved participants from Him. Let's have a brief lesson in Christian Marriage-ology.

I have to believe that an all-wise God who handcrafted man and woman in His own image, and then instituted and ordained marriage must have had a purpose in doing so. Would you agree? To find out the purpose, we must go to the place where all of God's thoughts, intents and views on everything are documented: the Holy Bible.

For the most part, Christian authors and theologians alike have run into incredible difficulty in actually clarifying what God's purpose for marriage is. Numerous books have been dedicated to offering advice on how to save, grow or even end a marriage. Others assist by describing the marital roles and general assigned operational tasks within a marriage but it is difficult to find many pages that offer the explanation for God's purpose for marriage.

I propose the following as a consideration of three of God's intentions for marriage; God's purpose for marriage is functional, sacramental and finally transformational or sanctifying.

MARRIAGE'S FUCTIONAL PURPOSE
The Bible gives us a three-fold purpose of marriage. First, there is the purpose of companionship; secondly, that of procreation; and third, that of sexual fulfillment as they are both preserved in chastity until marriage, demonstration of God's glory - sacrament.

Marriage involves man and woman being fitted together for the purposeful function of mutual fellowship, encouragement and understanding; the reproduction of children; and the physical and spiritual aspects of sexual satisfaction.

COMPANIONSHIP
Companionship was the one thing lacking for Adam amidst all the wonders of the Edenic creation while it was still "uncursed" before the first sin of mankind. The heavens, the earth, the oceans, the fishes of the sea, the creatures on the land and luscious fruit of the trees could not supply man with companionship, so marriage was designed to fulfill that void. Genesis 2:18-25 illustrates the first portion of this "three-part" purpose in the example of God creating everything, He looked at His creation observationally

then expressed delight by saying, "It was good." He was pleased with all that He had made.

The only thing that God saw as "not good" in the garden was that man was alone. Adam was not literally alone because God's presence and the animals were in the garden with him. But he was alone in the sense that he did not have adequate companionship that could relate to him in the way that he needed. So God then created the woman, Eve, as a wife and companion for him. She would be Adam's "help-meet," to meet his personal needs and assist him in fulfilling his responsibilities of overseeing the community.

CHILDBEARING AND SEXUAL PLEASURE

This purpose is supported in Genesis 1:28. God mandated that mankind should have many children. He said, "Be fruitful and multiply!" He further instructs us to replenish the earth.

Procreation is a rather large purpose of marriage in that God created it as a means for Christ to come as Redeemer. Sex, which God created solely for marriage, is not only for the purpose of procreation but for satisfying our natural sexual desires and the fulfillment of sexual needs to prevent sin (1 Corinthians 7:2).

Another purpose for marriage is one of sacrament. The main meaning of marriage is to display the covenant-keeping love between Christ and his church. In other words, God designed marriage most deeply and most importantly to be a parable or a drama of the way Christ loves his church and the way the church loves and follows Christ. As long as a couple is married they continue to display—however imperfectly—the ongoing commitment between Christ and his church.

In Ephesians 5:31, which is the basis for this argument, says (as also stated in Genesis 2:24 and Mark 10:7), "For this reason a man will leave his father and mother and will be joined to his wife, and the two will become one flesh," and then he gives us his interpretation of this Old Testament writing in verse 32, "This mystery is great—but I am saying that it refers to Christ and the church."

In other words, it is feasible to interpret Paul's words as saying that marriage (the covenant involved in leaving father and mother and being united to a spouse) is patterned after Christ's covenant commitment to his church. Upon this interpretation, Christ thought of Himself as the bridegroom coming for his bride, the church. According to Matthew 9:15 and John 3:29, Paul recognized his ministry as gathering the bride. He also indicates the same in 2 Corinthians 11:2 stating: "For I am jealous for you with a Godly jealousy, because I promised you in marriage to one husband to present you as a pure virgin to Christ."

The most ultimate thing we can say about marriage is that it exists for God's glory. That is, it exists to display God. Now, after looking at the passage in Ephesians, we can see how marriage is patterned after Christ's covenant relationship to the church—it's consistent and everlasting. Therefore, the highest meaning and most ultimate purpose of marriage is to put the covenant relationship of Christ and his church on display.

Marriage is therefore essential, mysterious and magnificent because it points to something essential, mysterious and magnificent. The love that binds husband and wife—even the first husband and wife before the fall—is a glorious love because it portrays the never-ending love that Christ has for us. According to this divine purpose for marriage, the greatest aspect and function of marriage is it displays something unspeakably great, love.

Let's look at the purpose of sanctification. What if God had an end in mind that went beyond our happiness, comfort and desire to be infatuated (in our marriage)? What if God designed marriage to make us holy more than to make us happy?

Scriptural substantiation for this purpose of marriage is also found in Ephesians 5. This time, however, the exposition of the text, verses 15-33, is focused not on the illustration that marriage should demonstrate Christ-likeness. The role of a husband requires one to sacrificially love their wife as Christ loved the church and came in all humility to die for her and the role of the wife requires one to humbly submit to her husband, relinquishing herself as top priority.

Philippians Chapter 2 is also support for this divine purpose for marriage, which recognizes God's intentions with this institution to shape and mold His people into becoming the servant-rulers that all Christians should strive to be.

This idea of marriage states that we completely deny ourselves and our selfish ambitions for the sake of considering others more important than ourselves. Marriage calls us to an entirely new and selfless life—a 24--hours-a-day, 7-days-a-week service commitment that acts as a crucible grinding and shaping us into the character of Jesus Christ.

I would say the first three years of marriage are by far the most difficult because it is the time when two previously separate individuals are learning to become one person. They are shedding selfish ways to adopt another's way of living. There is no more personal space as now what's his is yours and what's yours is his. This unifying process forces you to address your personal character issues as someone else is now holding you personally accountable for all of your behavior. This lifetime commitment of providing emotional, physical and spiritual intimacy, as well as care for another, uncovers who you are as your true self. You can't hide anymore! The truth about you will definitely be revealed.

Marriage is a God-glorifying, God-ordained institution that was created with the main purpose of conforming us into the holy image of Christ. The joys, difficulties and challenges of marriage serve as crucibles to refine our character and strengthen our faith in and knowledge of God. So, God's primary purpose of marriage, in line with one of His primary purposes for us living in this depraved world, is to transform others and ourselves into the likeness of His Son through our marriage experience.

BECOMING ONE FLESH

The teachings of the bible are divided into those that deal with rules and the Commandments handed down to the Children of Israel and those that deal with God's mercy and forgiveness, the Gospel. The former is called the Law. The major purpose of the Law in the Bible is to uncover sin and lead men to acknowledge it before God. That being said, we must look at God's ultimate plan as revealed in the Gospel, which is the Good News about Christ. Christian marriage was designed by God to be a reflection of this Good News. To understand this a bit better, let's turn to what the Apostle Paul said in Ephesians 5:22-30:

> "Wives submit to your husbands as to the Lord. For the husband is the head of the wife as Christ is the head

of the church, his body, of which he is the Savior. Now as the church submits to Christ, so also wives should submit to their husbands in everything."

"Husbands, love your wives, just as Christ loved the church and gave himself up to her to make her holy, cleansing her by the washing with water through the word, land to present her to himself as a radiant church, without stain or wrinkle, or any other blemish, but holy and blameless. In this same way, husbands ought to love their wives as their own bodies. He who loves his wife loves himself. After all, no one ever hated his own body, but he feeds and cares for it, just as Christ does the church—for we are members of His body."

How important it is that we understand the implications of that passage in defining marriage. When husband and wife love Jesus deeply, they understand that Jesus has made them members of His body, the church. They are committed to being completely unified or becoming "one flesh" as it relates to both our bond to God and within our earthly marriage. We should be one in marriage, even though from time to time the relationship may be strained. We must know that God forgives our failures in Christ and thus learn to forgive one another, consistently, without judgment or bringing the past forgotten "sins" into the present.

This is how Christ loves and how we should love each other in our marriages. This is the deeper meaning of our Christian marriages. We bear witness to the Gospel, the good news, by demonstrating this type of unbroken fellowship and spiritual unity within our relationships. The one flesh union points beyond itself to the union we have in Christ. Thus believing wives submit to their husbands, as to the Lord, and believing husbands love their wives just as Christ loved the church and gave himself up for her to make her holy. In this manner, they both reflect the grace that we all receive in Christ. The marriage should also bear fruit—their children should be raised, protected and taught to follow their example demonstrating Godly love and unity in faith with others.

MARRIAGE ROLES AND ASSIGNMENTS

A good indication of how you will fare in marriage is how you operate as a part of a team with people very different than yourself or within a supportive role in the church or on the job. How easy are you to get along with? How helpful are you to others? How faithful are you to your assignments at work? How forgiving are you when others grieve you? How well do you communicate when your needs are not being met? How well do you resolve conflict? How well do you follow commands and support the leadership without strife, bickering, or complaining? Do you easily submit to orders? Oh no, the "S" word… Submission!

The truth is, if you have difficulty being comfortable in the scenarios presented above and are not "successful" following instructions from your boss on the job, then you probably do not want to get married. In the hierarchy of marriage, the husband is basically our immediate supervisor, or spiritually speaking, he is your pastor. Ideally, the husband would be a great leader, a man that provides, who takes control in the role of headship, who makes good decisions for his household, teaches his children the correct way to go, nurtures, develops and brings out the best in his wife and children. In this case, ladies, submission to great leadership happens effortlessly. But oh how frustrating it is to try to submit to a man who is not properly leading? It is VERY frustrating and downright emotionally and mentally draining, so you want to prevent this situation from occurring by selecting mates who are good leaders.

Submission is actually a beautiful thing, especially when it is done as the Bible outlines it. Lots of people have a warped perspective on submission, meaning they understand submission to only go one way—the wife submits to the husband, does whatever he says no matter what, and she just speaks when spoken to and not otherwise.

This distorted view of submission would then depict the wife as a piece of property that transfers with the wedding ceremony, and she is good for cooking, making babies and doing whatever else the man feels comfortable "letting her do." Her skills, talents and ministry gifts are often closeted for fear that the husband will not get all of the shine. She is not free to give insight or wisdom to her husband regarding major life decisions that affect their family. She is not allowed to give wisdom regarding poor-decision making on behalf of the husband because "The man is in charge and the woman submits." This is a misrepresentation of biblical submission, and if couples would follow the correct outline for mutual submission, the marriage would be more likely to experience success in all areas as both parties are equally responsible to the other for support.

A prudent wife adds favor to her husband and her actual role assignment is to be a "help-meet" or what the Bible defines as a "helper suitable" to her husband. How can the wife help her husband meet the demands of leadership if the husband has a faulty perspective on submission and feels that he shouldn't or won't listen to his wife in the marriage?

This is why extensive communication regarding the topic is

so important prior to marriage. Having a partner who does not believe in mutual submission will derail both of your destinies, as you both will not be allowed to operate in your proper role assignments per God's instructions.

MUTUAL SUBMISSION

Yes, I'm still talking about submission!. God's will is for Christians to esteem His entire Word, and to both understand it and obey it in biblical balance. However, all too often Christians fail either to understand biblical balance in marriage roles or are simply not willing to obey God.

God has given five basic principles for marriages that are to be obeyed, not because a husband or wife "feels like it," and not because the other person "deserves it," but because God commands our obedience.

Godly submission can be somewhat difficult if you do not have a Godly husband. That's why it is crucial that you not marry an unbeliever, as it makes it all the more difficult to follow Godly principles with a mate who does not know God, understand God, or care about Godly living. The result of marrying an unbeliever is that you basically enter into a life-long tug-a-war with each other and God. You will be forced to constantly make decisions that require that you consistently weigh trying to obey God or obey your ungodly husband when his instructions to you conflict with the ways of God. Trust me—this is an unnecessary war that you definitely do not want to put yourself in.

You need a husband who not only understands God with his mind and states that he loves God with his mouth, but also proves that he does by leading his family in living Godly principles.

With an unbelieving husband, it becomes that wife's responsibility to "win him over to God" by her lifestyle (1Cor 7:17 and 1 Peter3:1). The Word basically says in these texts that an unbelieving husband is won by the Christ-like behavior of his wife-her purity, gentle quiet spirit of kindness and consistent forgiveness. The wife becomes the closest example to the unbelieving husband of what God is like and potentially a great witness to him. At the same time, the challenges that come along with being married to an unbeliever make it ten times harder to "be Christ-like" because of the conflicts that arise from two people who are living together and in essence are on two different paths. Making that kind of relationship work in general is tough—it is easier when both people in a relationship have similar views about life, family and God.

UNDERSTADING THE MARRIAGE ROLES
If a wife is to be obedient to God, she must first understand her God-given role in society and the family. In our post-Christian culture with its rejection of divine revelation and ethical absolutes, women have become increasingly misguided in this area.

The God-given urge for family and children still exists. However, this creational reality is sublimated to an autonomous, sinful, hedonistic, selfish view of life. Many women in this day and age put off marriage and children into the distant future to concentrate on careers, fun and sexual fulfillment. Even marriage itself has been redefined -it is no longer seen as a glorious God-ordained method of serving Christ's kingdom. It is now viewed as a purely human interaction that is convenient for increasing romance and/or one's selfish needs. When the relationship is no longer "romantic" or "fulfilling," one's partner is generally cast aside even though the children in the family will suffer for many years, perhaps a lifetime, from the parent's decisions to divorce each other.

Given the importance of wives and mothers in God's plan for society and culture, and God's impending judgment for the world's rejection of His Word, we should take marriage more seriously. Women must seek God for our true purpose and understand our importance in the family-marriage. Wives only will find true freedom when they believe in Christ and submit their lives to God's plan for the family.

As we study the duties of the wife, we must keep in mind that although many commands are directed to wives in scripture, husbands are still responsible for the behavior of their wives. This means that husbands have a responsibility to make sure that all members of the family understand their biblical duties and put those duties into practice.

BIBLICAL INSTRUCTIONS TO WIVES:
LET'S EXAMINE THREE MAIN AREAS OF INSTRUCTION TO THE WIVES.

First, the central command to wives is to be subject to their own husbands or to submit to their husbands. Paul writes: "Wives, submit to your own husbands, as to the Lord. For the husband is head of the wife, as also Christ is head of the church; and He is the Savior of the body. Therefore, just as the church is subject to Christ, so let the wives be to their own husbands in everything. Nevertheless let each one of you in particular so love his own wife as himself, and let the wife see that she respects her husband" (Ephesians 5:22-24, 33).

The word hupotassesthe, translated as "submit" in verse 22, is a present middle imperative of hypotass. This verb when used in the military means to place or rank under. When it is used by Paul in the middle voice, it means "to subject one's self, to obey, to submit to one's control, and to yield to one's admonition or advice." Christian wives are commanded to submit to the authority of their own husbands in the Lord. The same command is repeated in Colossians 3:18, "Wives, submit to your own husbands, as is fitting in the Lord." The expression "as is fitting" (hsanken) means that the submission of the wife to her own husband is appropriate Christian behavior. The apostle clearly expects every professing Christian wife to immediately begin to submit to their own husbands in the Lord, the moment they become a believer. Submission on the part of the wife to her own husband is not optional, but is a necessary aspect of Christian behavior.

THE "S" WORD: WHAT DOES "SUBMISSION" REALLY MEAN?

When the topic of submission comes up among women and men, the conversation is quite interesting to say the least. What does submission really mean for women? Does it mean that women are inferior to men? Does submission only work in one direction, where the men do not have to do anything?

Adam was created first; Eve was created second and originated from him, which leads directly to the next reason for the submission of the wife. Eve was created for her husband to be a helpmate or as one of the original translations of the word states, "help-meet" unto him. The creation narrative reads: "And the LORD God said, 'It is not good that man should be alone; I will make a helper comparable to him'"(Gen 2:18). The placement of this verse in the creation account is very significant. Immediately after verse 18 it says (in verses 19 to 20) that God brought all the animals to Adam to see what he would call them. In the Bible, names are generally assigned to animals (and people) with a specific purpose and on the basis of their potential demonstration of character.

For Adam, naming the animals was not arbitrary but based on empirical observations and careful analysis. Assigning names to each creature was a scientific endeavor if you will because as all the animals passed before him, he would examine them closely, then after careful thought, he would assign them a name. During this time of study and reflection, Adam became very aware that seeing all of creation, he was unique. In every species except man, there was both male and female. It is likely that at this time, Adam realized that he was incomplete in and of himself, that he needed a mate, a female counterpart. God providentially enabled Adam to understand his incompleteness and "prepared him" to meet his wife.

Adam's need of a wife, is clearly seen in the dominion mandate:

> "So God created man in His own image; in the image of God He created him; male and female He created them. Then God blessed them, and God said to them, 'be fruitful and multiply; fill the earth and subdue it; have dominion over the fish of the sea, over the birds of the air, and over every living thing that moves on the earth'"(Gen. 1:27-28).

God gives two assignments to Adam and Eve: procreation and

dominion. Adam and Eve are given the responsibility to develop a worldwide, God-glorifying culture! They are given dominion over the creatures for their development under God. It is obvious that Adam could not fulfill the assignment without a wife. Procreation and the raising of children (a godly seed) are necessary to fill up the earth. The wife plays an essential role as a "help-meet" in the task of dominion.

I've used the word "help-meet" often in this book. In the chapter about having "suitable help" the ideas is that with suitable help both persons in the marriage union arrive at destiny because their partner "helps" then to do so. The pair complements each other, to form a perfect whole, a harmonious team. The man and the woman are different; yet these differences are designed by God to "fit together" like a jig-saw puzzle or in a manner as to make the two stronger and more effective together than if they were apart. Adam and Even needed each other. Unlike the messages that society tends to send about the importance of wives in the family, the story of the creation of Eve exalts the role of wife and mother.

IMPLICATIONS OF SUBMISSION

The Bible is crystal clear in teaching that the wife has a different role in the marriage relationship. Although created in the image of God and equal to the man ontologically, the wife was created as a helper to the man. This teaching has many implications for understanding the roles of husbands and wives.

As previously stated, women are to assist their husband in the task of Godly dominion. The husband is to glorify God and extend dominion over the earth by means of his calling in life and the wife is to help her husband be the best he can be (in a biblical manner) in his particular calling. This means that the wife's "career" and calling in life is not found outside the home but is centered on her husband and children. This is not to say that a wife should not have a career or life outside of her husband and home, but once you become married, being a wife is your primary job. Your main focus should entail being an exceptional wife and mother, and all other things should be prioritized after that. Prioritizing and balancing life's responsibilities are crucial for wives. If you are unwilling or unable to dedicate the best of yourself to the success of your family by prioritizing your future husband, children and household needs before friends, family and career goals, then you may not want to get married. This is, however, the basic role or job description of a wife.

There usually is a natural God-given urge for women to get married, bear children and manage their homes. "To rule the house," means as the wife and mother in the home, you manage the household affairs. Not taking care of this major responsibility is out of order. Your priority over running businesses, ministries or helping others is to make sure that your home is functioning properly and the needs of your family are being met. I believe that you can have it all—a successful marriage, family life and career; proper prior preparation prevents poor performance to do so.

In my situation-with the current demands of my life, I will need to make certain mental and literal adjustments before I marry to assure that my life is conducive to managing a family. I'm single right now —I go and come as I please without any restraints, but I'll need to plan to include others when married. Although I plan to continue to travel in business and ministry, once I have a family I will need to plan business and ministry first around the needs of my family. I must make sure that my house is in order and that my first assignment, of a wife, is being effectively completed before I take on other tasks outside of my home.

OBEDIENCE AS UNTO GOD

Although most people do not like it, everyone has to be obedient to someone else in some form or another. We all must follow instructions in life—those of our parents, societal laws, employers, etc. This establishes order and structure for everyone. The same is true for marriage relationships. People often "obey," "serve" and "submit" in the world- in their jobs and ministries much more willingly than to their spouses in their marriages for some reason.

Single Wives must prepare their minds for marriage. You have to have the right attitude about the real-life expectations of your future marriage; the focus is no longer about you and what you want all of the time anymore. You must begin to learn how to effectively communicate and negotiate with your spouse. There is an old wise saying that, "You can catch more bees with honey than vinegar." There is a way to express yourself and get what you want from your mate, but it does not include yelling, screaming and being mean to do it. That is childish. It is also important that wives do not manipulate their husbands to get their own way. A wife who manipulates her husband by crying, nagging, complaining or making deals is not fulfilling her role as a wife. For example, I'll do this if you let me do that, etc., or begging or even intimidation, which may include, "I will not be a happy wife if I do not get such and such…" is obviously not fulfilling the spirit of this requirement. That type of behavior is deceitful, disrespectful and domineering. When the apostle Peter discusses the submission of the wife he notes the importance and beauty "of a gentle and quiet spirit" (1 Pet. 3:4). A woman's outward adornment and behavior should reflect a Godly, submissive interior character. Obviously a woman who is self-willed, manipulative and plotting does not fulfill this requirement.

The submission of the wife to her husband is to be done in a respectful manner. Wives are commanded to respect their husbands. "Let the wife see that she respects her husband" (Eph. 5:33).

R-E-S-P-E-C-T

A wife's respect for her husband should be displayed in both what a wife does not do and what a wife does toward her husband. Respect involves many things that a wife must avoid in her speech and behavior. Wives should never submit to their husbands with anger, stubbornness, irritation, grouchiness, nagging, complaining, smart remarks and so on. Wives should not criticize their husbands by saying their decisions are stupid, wrong or unwise. A respectful attitude does not focus on a husband's defects.

When a husband does make a mistake, a respectful wife will not rub it in with a "See, I told you so." Also, a wife should never make comments that are intended to hurt her spouse and tear him down. Telling a husband that he doesn't make enough money, or that she shouldn't have married him, or that if she had been more patient she could have found a better spouse, is clearly off-limits.

Respect also involves a proper attitude and speech when the wife is away from home. This means that Christian wives do not criticize or put down their husbands in front of others—parents, friends, acquaintances, strangers or anyone. Even if a wife's remarks are 100% true she must never tear down her husband's reputation before others. She should speak to her husband privately, humbly and respectfully about his problems.

If his problems cannot be dealt with privately then biblical counseling is needed with his consent. Obviously if sin is involved, Matthew 18:15 comes into play, which basically says that, "if your brother sins against you, go to him and let him know, attempt to resolve the conflict" (emphasis added). Women's groups and Bible studies that allow gossip and disrespect to spouses must be avoided. Women must respect their husbands even in their absence. They should not even make disparaging remarks about their spouses to their children.

A wife who shows disrespect to her husband behind his back to others is simply feeding her own bitterness and disrespect instead of dealing with the alleged offense biblically. "Whoever hides hatred has lying lips, and whoever spreads slander is a fool. In the multitude of words sin is not lacking, but he who restrains his lips is wise" (Proverbs 10:18-19). A Christian wife should focus on good positive things regarding her husband when talking to others. The husband who is respected can trust his wife with others." The heart of her husband safely trusts her; so he will have no lack of gain. She does him good and not evil all the days of her life" (Proverbs 31:11-12)." An excellent wife is the crown of her husband, but she who causes shame is like rottenness in his bones" (Proverbs 12:4). Think about that.

Respect is not merely avoiding certain behaviors. A wife must show respect to her husband by complimenting and building him up. As a help meet, she is to encourage him in his God-given calling. Even when the husband does a good job mowing the lawn or building a shed, the wife should compliment his work. When a wife respects her husband biblically she helps him do more for the kingdom of God and their family. There is an element of truth in the phrase that it is a woman who makes the man because a man who is married to a Godly wife can often attain a greater level of sanctification and achievement.

When wives are told that they must respect their husbands, they often raise the following questions: "Yes, that is what the Bible says, but, what if my husband does not deserve respect? What should I do then?" The Scriptures teach us that the wife must still respect her husband. The respect of the wife is not contingent upon the respectability of the husband. How do we know that the wife's respect is not to be dependent upon the respectability of the husband? Well, the command to respect comes with no qualifications or expectations. The Bible teaches that the respect of the wife toward her husband is the best method of rendering him respectable. If a woman is married to an unbeliever or a mediocre Christian, she must find ways to respect her husband. Her submissive, respectful attitude can be used of God to win over a stubborn husband to Christ.

The idea that women should show disrespect to poor leaders or unbelieving husbands is not supported in the Bible. On the contrary, he says that submission, respect and inner beauty is the best method for converting unsaved husbands. The respect shown is actually directed toward God and His authority, and not fundamentally toward the man in who it is invested." When a woman's life corresponds to her verbal witness, her words are far more effective. When a believing wife is married to a Christian who is sloppy in his walk, who is a poor leader, the best thing she can do for his sanctification is to be respectful, and submissive. Godliness on the part of the wife is used by God to convict and sanctify the husband.

Another faulty belief of some Christian women is that respect and submission only should be given as a reward for respectability and love on the part of the husband. There are woman who are in such situations who will outwardly obey a husband's instructions yet do so with a respectful, bitter spirit. They believe that they must punish their husband's bad behavior in order to see positive change. This type of attitude not only violates 1 Peter 3:1-6, but also the teaching of Paul that we are never to fight evil with more evil. He says, "Do not be overcome by evil, but overcome evil with good" (Rom. 12:21). The wife is to declare war on her husband and attempt to take him captive for Christ. However, the weapons she uses are obedience, respect, gentleness, and quietness to win. His basic strategy is to overcome his evil by doing good...such submission is not dogmatism. It is aggressive and violent submission. No Christian wife needs to sit still in tough marital situations- doing so would be sinful. God has given the marching orders-"Overcome evil with good"!

MOTIVATION OF OBEDIENCE

We must understand that the motivation for obedience is not one's feelings but a desire to please Jesus Christ. Our motivation must always be Christ-centric. Even if a woman desires to please God by being submissive, she will not always feel like being submissive. Also in a conflict, when feelings are intense, it may be difficult for her to submit. Regardless of her feelings, she should honor Christ by developing a mindset or a resolve to do the right thing in the right way with the right motive whether she feels like it or not. In the process, her feelings will eventually improve and God works miracles in our situations when we trust and obey Him.

When a husband does not feel respected, it usually causes him to "act out" because his innermost need is not being met by his wife. He will feel depressed or angry and will purposely avoid his wife. He will stay longer at the office or go off by himself engaging in hobbies or watching TV rather than spending time with you. This behavior in turn will lead the wife to have even less respect for her husband. She may begin to nag him and treat him worse than before which creates a very dysfunctional cycle between the two. Such a woman is literally tearing down her household by her disobedience. Ideally, the Christian husband (who is both the leader and is ultimately responsible for what occurs in the home) would lead and communicate with his wife to resolve the conflicts in such a situation. However, if he does not lead biblically or effectively, Peter says that wives are to turn things around by their respectful Godly behavior. Wives are not to wait until their husbands get their act together. They are to take the initiative. They are to obey and build up their house. "Every wise woman builds her house, but the foolish pulls it down with her own hands" (Proverbs 14:1).

OTHER WIFELY DUTIES
Being a good wife involves many duties and responsibilities as you have seen in the previous sections. In this section, we will

consider some of the duties that are more commonly discussed and are also very important to sustaining healthy marriages.

BEING A SOUL MATE

One of the main reasons that God created Eve was for Adam to have meaningful companionship. "And the Lord God said, 'It is not good that man should be alone; I will make him a helper comparable to him'" (Genesis 2:18). Adam could have had animals, such as a dog or cat, as companions. However, in such a case he would have still been alone in a sense because animals cannot engage in meaningful conversation. Eve was created as a helper suitable for the him. A wife is there not merely to keep house, raise children and satisfy her husband sexually, but she also is to be her husband's soul mate. It is very important that husbands and wives communicate about all areas of life on a daily basis. They both need to be there for each other, to encourage, comfort, give praise, laugh, cry and so on. It is wise for husbands and wives to set time aside for good conversation. It can occur over dinner, a pleasant walk or simply sitting around the family room after dinner. If a woman is married to a man who is not talkative or is distant, she must communicate her need of biblical companionship. Husbands and wives may not have the same hobbies or secular interests. They do, however, have children and the Lord Jesus Christ to talk about. These are great areas to generate interesting and edifying conversation for an eternity. Be a meaningful companion to your spouse.

WALKING WITH EACH OTHER IN KNOWLEGE AND UNDERSTANDING

Christian husbands and wives are "heirs together of the grace of life" (1 Peter 3:7). Their task of Godly dominion now has a redemptive focus. This means that their companionship is to be directed toward mutual satisfaction. This involves family worship, praying for each other, theological discussion and mutual admonishment. Husbands and wives are in a unique position of knowing virtually every intimate detail about the other. In doing so, they not only can pray for each other according to knowledge, but they can lovingly point out each other's sins and faults to help the other grow spiritually. When married couples have a close biblical relationship, they are not defensive regarding this type of communication, but it is encouraged. If a husband has a behavior that is offensive to others and he may not be aware, then he should be thankful to his wife for pointing this out to him and assisting him to improve his character.

CHILDBEARING

The wife, if able, is to provide her husband with children. Wives should not succumb to the modern secular humanistic propaganda that says that children are a nuisance to be avoided or that the world is overpopulated. God commanded fruitfulness to Adam and Eve as an aspect of worldwide dominion. "Then God blessed them, and said, 'be fruitful and multiply [Hebrew, rabah – "to increase exceedingly"]; fill the earth and subdue it'" (Genesis. 1:28). This command is repeated after the fall to Noah and his sons also (Gen. 9:1). The Holy Spirit says specifically through the prophet Malachi that one of the purposes of marriage is to provide a godly offspring. "Yet she is your companion and your wife by covenant...to create godly offspring (Malachi. 2:14 emphasis added). Unlike our modern post-Christian culture, the Bible always views an abundance of covenant children as a great blessing. "Behold, children are a heritage from the Lord, the fruit of womb is a reward. Like arrows in the hand of a warrior, so are the children of one's youth. Happy is the man who has his quiver full of them" (Psalms. 127:3-5).

God commands believing husbands and wives to "greatly multiply", says that He seeks a godly seed, and teaches that an abundance of covenant children is a great blessing, so why would professing Christians limit their family size to two or three children? Could it be that Evangelical and Reformed churches have been influenced by our anti-family, anti-children culture? Could it be that many modern believers are more interested in material pursuits (e.g., fancy houses, shiny new cars, exotic vacations, new clothes, etc.) rather than filling up a quiver full of children for the purpose of godly dominion? It is simply a matter of obedience to the clear teaching of Scripture. When biological reproduction is not an option due to medical reasons, then foster parenting and adoption are great options as there are many children all around the world who need a safe home and good parents.

SEXUAL FULFILLMENT:
PREPARING TO MEET HIS NEEDS

A wife has a biblical obligation to be there for her husband sexually:

> 1 Cor. 7:2-5 reads, "Nevertheless, because of sexual immorality, let each man have his own wife, and let each woman have her own husband. Let the husband render to his wife the affection due her, and likewise also the wife to her husband. The wife does

not have authority over her own body, but the husband does. And likewise the husband does not have authority over his own body, but the wife does. Do not deprive one another except with consent for a time, that you may give yourselves to fasting and prayer; and come together again so that Satan does not tempt you because of your lack of self-control".

This verse teaches us that one of the purposes of marriage is to protect both husband and wife from sexual immorality. This point was very important for believers in Greek and Roman society with their rampant sexual immoralities and perversions and it is equally important in our sex-obsessed culture.

The Christian wife must take the responsibility of fulfilling her husband's sexual needs seriously. Apart from the period of the menstrual cycle (Lev. 20:18; Ez. 18:5-6) and mutually agreed upon times of prayer and fasting (1 Cor. 7:15), the wife should never refuse her husband's advances. It is not enough, however, that the wife simply participates in the act in a robotic way. She must give herself to her husband in a happy, warm, affectionate and joyful manner. The husband should sense happiness and joy from his wife and not get the impression that she feels that sex is a nuisance or that she should like to hurry up and get it over with.

In our goal to be obedient to Christ, the wife must learn to set aside personal issues, other concerns like work, and focus her attention on giving her husband the joyful, meaningful, fantastic sexual pleasure that should be a part of every biblical marriage. The husband must also put his wife first in this area by picking times when the wife will not be distracted by stressors. A wife who neglects this area and refuses to fulfill her responsibility is behaving in a manner that is leading her husband into temptation. This area requires diligence.

For those who have been married for any length of time and have children will understand that fulfilling this responsibility is not always an easy task. There are hormonal changes associated with childbirth that can drastically reduce a woman's libido and taking care of small children can be exhausting-physically and mentally. Further, some women have a decreased sexual drive as they age and go through menopause. All of these aspects of life can lead wives to want to have sex less frequently. What can be done about these common experiences by Christian wives? The wife should be open and honest about these things and ask her husband for help and understanding- talk often about each other's sexual desires and consistently work on furling them in creative ways to make it more pleasurable despite life's stressors.

Proper planning is necessary in this area as well for those who have busy schedules. Perhaps the husband could set aside time for his wife to take a nap during the day. If there are hormonal problems they should research the problem and consult a doctor. The husband and wife must examine the various issues that may prevent them from having a vibrant sex life and make the necessary changes together so that both will heartily fulfill their marital responsibilities.

There should be no limitations (with reason) for married couples to keep the bedroom hot and steamy. The good book says, "Marriage is honorable among all, and the bed undefiled; but fornicators and adulterers God will judge" (Heb. 13:4). So, married couples should be having the hottest love-making ever! They should be the world's model for how to have sex; fun, adventurous and uninhibited romance and love-making. After all, sex was designed for marriage.

PRACTICING LOVE; TRUE LOVE - GOD'S LOVE
There are a few principles in practicing God's love in our singleness and marriages'; Obeying God, loving God and trusting God no matter how we feel. To understand God's command that "husbands love their wives", we must recognize that "love" is translated as "agape." By inserting the meaning of "agape," we paraphrase: "Husbands, each of you must dedicate yourself to your wife and to her good. You must purpose and do those things that are best for her, whether you like her or not, no matter how she treats you, even if it "kills you", just as Christ dedicated Himself to the church and gave His life for it" (Ephesians 5:25 emphasis added).

    We can shed further light on the husband's role in marriage by considering the thirteenth chapter of 1 Corinthians. The text is often quoted in wedding and talks about "charity" or "love,". Once again, we need to understand that God is speaking of "agape" love. Agape love does not seek its own desires or ways—it is not selfish (1 Corinthians. 13:5). Instead, agape love is directed toward the good of the other person. Therefore, for a husband to love his wife in accordance with God's command in Ephesians 5:25, he must unselfishly dedicate himself to doing what is best for his wife all the time. Agape love is not puffed up or proud (1 Corinthians 13:4). A husband does not love his wife as God has commanded him to do if he is so proud that he will not let his wife have a thought or an opinion that does not agree with his. By commanding that the wife submit to her husband, God has placed on husbands the responsibility for all decisions.

    Let's put the husband's leadership and the wife's submission in biblical balance:

> » God has given the husband the leadership role for the good of his wife, not as an excuse for him to be proud, selfish or to treat her as a servant. Some husbands do not seem to understand that yelling for food or beverage service while they are watching TV and their wives are scrubbing the kitchen floor on their hands and knees does not reflect biblical truth in balance.
>
> » God has not said the husband must, or should, make all decisions in his family. If a husband wants to please God, and if he loves his wife (with agape love), he will delegate some decision making to her in the overall management of their household because this would actually help him.
>
> » God has not said that the husband must make decisions without obtaining input from his wife because she has brains and wisdom to assist him to make good decisions.

SEEKING PEACE AT ALL TIMES

If the husband is not proud, he will not think that he is always right-he would have married an intelligent woman for a reason. If the husband is not selfish, he will not want his way but instead will desire to please his wife. God has not made him the leader in the family to feed his ego, or to satisfy his selfishness, but for her good.

So in understanding this, if the husband and wife disagree and he is not proud or selfish, then he will be willing to go along with her ideas and her desires at times for the sake of peace—unless it would hurt her or someone else spiritually, emotionally or physically. As a Godly husband, he should obey God and love his wife with agape love by assuming his God-given responsibilities of shielding his wife from undue emotional and physical loads that are too heavy for her. If a husband understands God's Word in biblical balance, he will not abdicate his God-given responsibilities to his wife, or for rearing their children.

God says that husbands must live with their wives "according to knowledge," giving [them] honor" (1 Peter 3:7) as the weaker vessel. Living with wives "according to knowledge" is much more than treating them with consideration. Living with wives according to knowledge includes: a) creating an atmosphere of absolute trust and they are able to reveal their deepest thoughts and feelings; b) gaining understanding through listening; and c) doing what is best for them in accordance with knowledge of their desires as a woman.

If the husband wants to obey God, please Him and show God that he loves Him, he will treat his wife with respect because God commands it.

I'd like to show how these principles relate to "being one." Too often, when "two become one," there is a power struggle to determine which "one" they will become. Will they become him? Or her? Instead of a selfish and prideful fight for power, they should become "one" in their desire to please God, in their desire to serve Him, in their desire to fulfill their respective roles in marriage and in their desire to help each other become more and more Christ-like.

Marriage can be likened to two trees. The husband should be like the oak tree. He is to be stronger, and to protect his wife from the winter winds. She is to be like the apple tree, not as strong but with a Godly beauty, usefulness and fragrance. If two trees are too close together, they do not have limbs all of the way around. If a husband loves his wife biblically, he will give her opportunity, space and encouragement to develop.

If a husband loves his wife as Christ loved the church and gave Himself for it, he will allow her, give her opportunity and encourage her, to develop as a competent woman in the home, in the church, and in the community. Proverbs 31:10-31 speaks of the wife having many virtues inside and outside of the home. She was a businesswoman, she heard of a field that was for sale, she considered its worth, and she bought it (verse 16).

There is a message for virtuous women about the desired characteristics of a husband in this same chapter of Proverbs. We read: "Her husband is known in the gates, when he sits among the elders of the land" (verse 23). Apparently, her reputation, and his reputation for his wisdom in using her skills and talents, had led him to a place of leadership in the community—he sat at the gate as one of the rulers. If a man is wise, he will take his wife as a full partner not only to help himself, but to help her develop her talents. If he really loves her, as opposed to considering her as a possession to serve his every desire, he will dedicate himself to playing a central role in her development in all areas of her life.

Wives submit? If a husband is loving her as God intends him to love her, he will be so unselfish and humbly dedicated to her good that submission to him will happen effortlessly. He'll be so considerate of God's will for her as well as her wishes, desires and opinions, that submission will be pleasurable and fulfilling. This is the beauty of the biblical roles in marriage. If biblical truth is held in balance and practiced, the husband will be dedicated to doing good for her, and she will gratefully support him in his leadership.

ARE YOU A WIFE?
"HE WHO FINDS A WIFE FINDS A GOOD THING AND OBTAINS FAVOR OF THE LORD." (PROVERBS 18:22)

Every married woman is not a wife. Unfortunately, having a wedding ceremony and wearing a ring on the designated finger on your left hand doesn't make a person a wife. There are wives that are actually "currently unmarried"-Single Wives.

As we have explored in this book, a wife exemplifies very specific virtues and Godly character in her singleness; she is destiny-driven and hold a distinct perspective about life in general-that is should be based "on purpose and in purpose". She thinks and operates distinctly differently from other women and thus her life demonstrates a certain caliber of excellence in all areas of her life. This level of dominion over her atmosphere, her mind, soul and body is necessary in being able to effectively function in her future role as a married wife because she understands the calling associated with this miraculous institution is great.

Are you a wife? Internal processing and personal action is required if you really wish to find out who you are, how developmentally mature you are and if you are really ready for marriage. You must fully acknowledge the truth and take responsibility for your life, no matter what state it is in. You will never arrive at Destiny until you take an honest look at where you currently are in relation to that goal and begin to take action to move beyond any perceived limitations or self-imposed restrictions and grow forward.

A WIFE IS
A wife is a suitable helper or a "help-meet" who will directly assist

her husband in meeting his God-given responsibilities in life. In order to effectively help someone else live at their highest potential and fulfill their life-assignments, it would make sense that they are fulfilling your God-ordained purpose and kingdom assignments as well.

News flash my sisters—being a help-meet does not mean that the wife is beneath the husband. At times a wife may be the stronger one in specific areas, but at other times she may be the weaker one in other areas. At times, you both may be on the exact same level in terms of strengths and weaknesses.

Wives have always demonstrated great ability to endure pain and hardship because of the strength that God has placed within her. The word help-meet or helpmate expresses the notion of complementarities. The wife is a helper matching or corresponding to her husband's level of need—she is suitable for him. Together, they make a perfect pair because they are both designed by God to complement one another to form a perfect whole, a harmonious team. The man and the woman are different; yet these differences are designed by God to enhance each other so that by the two working together they are stronger and more effective together than if they were apart.

GOD GIVES GOOD GIFTS

Wives are a "great good" or "good treasures" who deserve "great good" and "good treasures". When we are properly connected to God, operating in our purpose, and working on our God-given assignments we have demonstrated to God that our hearts are prepared to receive the kind of mind-blowing gift that God desires to give us. This proper alignment of our lives with purpose actually sets the scene for God to make the gift presentation to us of our mate. God gives awesome gifts that have the potential to change our entire lives for the better. These are the kinds of gifts that will usually cause rivalry or disruption in our attention to God once they are given to us, that's why He desires that you practice keeping Him first though intimate fellowship during your singleness as a pattern of living after He gives you the mind-blowing gift of your husband.

ARE YOU A GOOD GIFT?

God tests our readiness to receive such supernatural disruptions, Godly husbands, in our lives by how we operate in our relationship with Him as another person who will in fact take attention away from Him. We demonstrate our preparedness to have someone occupy the intimate space with Him by how we sacrificially offer ourselves to Him; mind, body and spirit during our singleness. We show Him through a life of worship and service to Him that we will not be easily swayed or moved from the core of our relationship with Him by the addition of "people and things" into our lives. Basically, He knows that we won't allow anything, even someone who we would love dearly to replace Him as an idol.

IS THE SCENE PREPARED FOR YOU TO BE PRESENTED?

When God actually created Eve from Adam's rib, the scene was set for her, as it should be for us when we are presented to our husbands. God had provided all that Adam needed to provide for his future wife, meaning Adam had an extremely intimate relationship with God and was fully dependent upon God for his daily provisions. He had an abundance of resources at his disposal and he had a job that he was accountable to God to complete.

Adam had a J.O.B. and was entirely capable of providing for Eve BEFORE she arrived on the scene.

REMOVING THE ROADBLOCKS

I believe that a part of my responsibilities as a married wife is to have my house together, both internally and externally. I should be organized, prepared to care for and manage the lives of those God will place in my life as my family. I must be a good cook, great mother, sexually appealing for my husband and physically, emotionally and spiritually prepared to create a strong home foundation for others to thrive in.

Unfortunately, I had some seemingly challenging roadblocks to creating this type of home foundation. Overcoming hopelessness, stagnation and emotional suspension was a consistent barrier to growth and it is a must if you ever plan to progress and live a superior life as a wife. True growth is painful at times, but remaining the same, year after year, is more painful—I call it a "slow death" actually because it goes against the natural pattern of life which is to grow, change, develop and progress.

My specific challenge was in my emotions-as a result I became somewhat addicted to food as a means to comfort myself. When I kept seeing the same weight loss goals in my journals year after year, it made me realize that I was not progressing or growing in the area of personal discipline necessary to achieve my body image goals. Looking at that goals that I hadn't been able to achieve which would ultimately benefit my personal health, made me feel like a complete failure on a very deep level. I spent too much time thinking about how I had disappointed myself and started to feel that I was directly standing in the way of me attracting my God-ordained mate; that made me feel "imprisoned"; helpless and hopeless.

A Godless life has no purpose, a purposeless life is meaningless, and a meaningless life is insignificant and hopeless".

TURNING MY HOUSE INTO A HOME
"A house is a building, but a home is a living organism". Have you heard the expression that "home is where the heart is?" A home is a place of peace, contentment, acceptance, rejuvenation, nurturing and love. Creating a home starts with the leadership or the builders of the home. Proverbs 14:1 tells us that, "a wise woman builds her house but a foolish woman destroys it with her own hand." Women build the foundation of the home. She is to be the heart of the home. She keeps it alive, thriving, beating on schedule and warm with love. She is the centerpiece that connects everyone else so she has to be healthy and connected to the source of life, God, to build her house effectively.

God had showed me a glimpse of my life with my God-ordained mate, my future husband, it was better than I could have ever imagined! He showed me that he was closer than I realized, and I felt an internal pressure to literally prepare, which was a good thing. I opened the door to the enemy, however, by waddling in a state of emotional stagnation wherein I focused on the few minor things that I had not accomplished on "my marriage preparation list" as opposed to the numerous wonderful personal feats that I had achieved. I allowed the enemy to play with my mind by depositing negative thoughts like, "See, that's why you don't deserve a good mate because you can't even organize your life," "you can't handle a husband and family because you are undisciplined...you have too much going on—your schedule is crazy, your house is a mess, you are completely overextended and you won't even commit to yourself to lose weight!"

I felt I was stuck in time—stagnant—and being held captive to myself by myself. How painful and internally frustrating this was, not to be able to make yourself do something that you really want to do. I felt like I hadn't adequately moved forward in this area in years. I had an internal war of the wills. My spirit desired to grow but my body wouldn't carry out those desires.

Spiritually speaking, it meant that I wasn't successful at bringing my body under subjection to my mind's instructions to eat properly and exercise regularly. So, I had to be honest about this situation-I couldn't do it on my own no matter how hard I had tried. I needed to allow God to help me. He did just that and by me inviting him in to help me accomplish my weight loss goals it was much easier than I had expected. God trained me in disciplining myself, Praise God! This principle of allowing God to help you to do those things that you are unable to do in your own power, work for every area of your life-even when it comes to being single wives or married wives.

TRAITS OF SINGLE WIVES

Just as there were specific notable characteristics listed for ideal mates or Godly husbands, we will also list them for you-Single Wives. In order to attract an ideal mate, you should be an ideal mate, so let's look at what the book of Proverbs has to say about virtuous women. Proverbs 31 is most specific with regard to the qualities of the Godly wife. These qualities are synonyms for being single wives:

- Always seeks to be Modest in Her Dress
- Always seeks to be Holy in Her Conduct
- Always seeks to be Truthful in Speech and Motives
- Seeks to be Gentle, Quiet and Peaceful
- Seeks to Care for the Home
- Seeks to Serve Others
- Strives to be a Person Who Can be Trusted
- Seeks to be Prudent in Financial Matters
- Seeks to be a Hard Worker
- Seeks to Do the Right Thing and Have a Good Reputation
- Seeks to Internalize Biblical Wisdom
- Seeks to Live Out the Truths of Womanhood by Applying Biblical Wisdom to Her Life
- Are Godly. Godliness begins with a Proper Relationship to God. A Godly Wife is, first and foremost, a Woman who Fears God.
- Wise. The wise woman builds her house, but the foolish tears it down with her own hands (14:1). She opens her mouth in wisdom and the teaching of kindness is on her tongue (31:26).
- Honorable gifts for potential husbands. A man who has married a godly wife has a wife who will bring honor to him. She is truly a helper to her husband.

An excellent wife is the crown of her husband but she who shames him is as rottenness in his bones (12:4). An ungodly wife humiliates and harasses her husband. She is not a helper but a hindrance to her mate. She is "as rottenness in his bones" (12:4). By her haranguing, she makes him miserable.

» Are Gracious. One reason honor is given to godly wives is because she is known for her graciousness. It is better to live in a corner of a roof, than in a house shared with a contentious woman (21:9; cf. 25:24). It is better to live in a desert land, than with a contentious and vexing woman (21:19).

» Faithful to their potential husbands. This is most clearly shown by contrast with the woman of folly who is an adulterous... "To keep you from the evil woman, from the smooth tongue of the adulteress" (6:24). While it is not stated explicitly, it is implied and assumed that a godly wife is one who maintains sexual purity. She is a woman who is virtuous or excellent (31:10), in whom her husband has complete trust (31:11). She does her husband only good and not evil (31:12). She teaches her son the virtues of sexual purity (31:3). Certainly she is a woman of sexual purity.

PREPARATION TO MEET HIS NEEDS

The woman must understand that God has designed man in such a way that sexual fulfillment is one of the most essential ways that he understands his mate's love for him. When a man marries his wife, he trusts her to meet his needs and sexual fulfillment is not simply a mere desire but a deep need designed by God for the male. A woman who fails to understand this is a thief and is robbing her mate of one of his most basic needs for the health of a relationship.

Sex often is taboo in the church, even when it is between married folks. Yet, sex seems to be being "had" among the churchgoers as indicated by the number of teen pregnancies. Pornography and adultery are major unspoken concerns among churchgoers and it would be helpful to have more open discussion about the underlining theme of sex.

In that same vein, Christian women need to get familiar with being sexy, being in shape for sex and open to doing whatever it takes to fulfill her husband's sexual needs as an adultery and divorce prevention strategy. I have been celibate for almost three years after my divorce, and I plan to have lots and lots of awesome sex and love making with my future husband. It has been a long time, but I'm preparing for that part of the marriage as well as getting in shape and staying current regarding this topic. As Christian women, we must become more secure in our sexual identity-comfortable with our bodies, open to being sexually adventurous and keeping ourselves up to remaining physically attractive. Having excellent self-esteem is essential to being sexually liberated and adventurous with your future husband.

REMAIN HIS HOMEGIRL AFTER THE WEDDING
"Be his homey, lover and friend…keep it fun like when you first met."

Men often complain because before they got married, their wives did many "fun" things with them. They would enjoy various spontaneous activities that were normal parts of their courting life. Sadly, when couples marry sometimes these activities dwindle away never to return.

Sometimes the woman makes the same mistake as the man in regards to affection. The man sometimes thinks since he has now married the woman that he has won her and the art of "winning her daily" through showing affection and love is now complete. Women sometimes do many activities with the man to show that she cares about him in the beginning-before marriage. Yet, when the two marry, the woman may feel as if all that is now less than important. Although we do not often feel this way, men do desire for their wives to be their closest companion in their endeavors, tasks and joys of life. A couple should learn how to find enjoyable activities that keep each other young and keep fun alive. Without this recreational companionship the marriage will definitely suffer.

BE STYLISH AND SEXY

Be hot and fabulous…don't let yourself go; ever prepare to live a lifestyle that would help you stay healthy and active. I've seen it happen too often. A single lady that is possibly overweight will work out in the gym, run, modify her diet to "get the man", then completely stop after she does. The things that you do to get him should be the things that you continue to do to keep him.

Work at presenting yourself a certain way, looking good and desirable. Make sure that when going on a date that you dress in such a way that will leave a memorable impression on your guy. I do not mean come dressed like a stripper, but be sexy and stylish in a classy way that creates a more lasting memory for your date. Guys are visual, but they really do not want to see all of your goods upfront (not the kind of guy that you should marry anyway). By showing him everything upfront, you leave nothing to his imagination! Part of the excitement during your dating and celibacy is your future husband eventually being able to "see" parts of you that he has imagined throughout your courtship.

Keep this same line of thinking after you guys' marry, keep him excited about seeing you and keep his imagination ignited sexually.

In cases where the woman neglects her body, appearance or other details to make herself attractive to her spouse she has become to some degree a liar. She wins him over with her presentation and other great qualities, then they marry, she lets her body go to waste, lets her appearance dwindle with little to no concern to please the senses and eyes of her mate. She has basically deceived her mate into thinking she would "be a certain way" or maintain her current appearance after the wedding. That is not fair. "Whatever you did to get him, you should continue doing to keep him."

HOLD DOWN THE HOUSEHOLD AND THE KIDS EFFICIENTLY

Hold down the household…if you do not cook, learn to cook, be able to clean or hire someone to do it. Make the home a pleasurable place, free from the hassles and stress of the world. Assure that the house is neat, clean and orderly. The children should be respectful and obedient to you both. This is important for the man's sanity. The holy women will seek to meet the most important areas of his needs. She will work to create a lovely home and environment where he may find peace because of her efforts. Now that we've gotten our houses in order, internally and externally, let's manifest our mates.

CHAPTER 5: MANIFESTING YOUR MATE. MIND MOUTH MANIFESTATION (MMM)

DESTINY DEPENDS ON YOUR DECISIONS...

Okay. We are almost there. You are now closer than ever to attracting your God-ordained mate and transitioning from Single Wives into Married Wives. I once again call your attention to the importance of dating only men that qualify as Godly husbands. You must be careful who you decide to allow into your life in general but be exceptionally careful as to who you choose for a marriage partner. Choosing the wrong mate can ultimately derail your destiny.

Now we know that "all things (eventually) work together for the good of them who love the Lord and are called according to His purpose, (Romans 8:28) but you do not want to waste any of your precious years recovering from mistakes and waiting to see the good in your poor decisions. Your time is valuable; use it wisely. Invest your dating time only on those who qualify as true friends and good leaders. True friends will aid you in fulfilling your purpose, reaching your God-potential and thus arriving at your Destiny moment sooner rather than later.

FIGHTING FEAR WITH FAITH
MIND-MOUTH-MANIFESTATION (MMM)

Faith says that I currently possess (in the spirit realm) the things that like I'll never acquire (in the natural realm). The things that I have in the spirit realm are brought to fruition in the natural realm though mind-mouth-manifestation or what I'll call "MMM". The things that I conceptualize in my mind, through visualization, and say aloud continuously (no matter how I feel), are the things that I will (eventually) see manifested into my life.

If you are not confessing daily, several times a day, what you believe, then you really do not believe it. The Word tells us that the proof of our believing something is what we say about it.

2 Corinthians 4:13 says, "In the same spirit of faith (the same spirit that God operated in when He created the world through MMM) according to that which is written, I believed and therefore I've spoken. We also believe and therefore we speak." (emphasis added). This is our example to follow for declaring into the atmosphere with Godly dominion what you believe or desire to create.

This model of MMM was given to us in Genesis 1:3, when God visualized the whole world in his mind in the mist of actually seeing complete and utter darkness-the world was empty and void. He used the MMM process to speak directly to the darkness or that was preventing what He wanted to see from manifesting, by saying, "Let there be light" or darkness let go of the light! And it happened just like He said. This is how we must deal with any seemingly resistant situation that is preventing us from experiencing our desires. We have the power and authority to call what we desire to see out of what we do not see. I call joy out of sadness, children out of barrenness, and a fruitfully blessed marriage out of my singleness based on the image of those things in my mind.

I believe in this process of MMM and I know that it will work for manifesting my marriage mate because I've seen it work in various other situations in my life. I am a woman of extreme faith and I operate in the gift of faith-the ability to hope against hope and pull the unseen things into the visible realm despite great physical adversity.

I remember a few years ago when I had been given permission to be released from my five-year marriage. I was emotionally crushed, humiliated and completely embarrassed because I had lost everything-I had also lost my dignity in a sense.

The things that I had lost, including my self-respect, made me angry with myself for putting myself in such a pitiful situation-one that could have been avoided. I hadn't, however, lost my faith or belief in God's Word. I still believed that His Word would prove true for me. Even with not a dime to my name, I still praised God and confessed the best for my life because that is what I saw in my mind; despite how I had mistreated myself over the years by settling, I still knew that I deserved the best in terms of relationships deep in my heart.

The economy was strained and not many opportunities presented themselves in terms of immediate employment. So then, I needed to get my business off the ground-quickly so that I would be able to provide for myself. I had no money. All of my bank accounts were in the negative. Although I have always had very supportive parents, I had prided myself since the age of 15 on working hard to take care of myself and to buy the things that

I needed so as not to be a burden to my parents. I did, however, return home with them to regroup and begin to rebuild my life. I'm so thankful for them. So, as a 30-year-old having to go back home to live with my parents after living on my own since college, I had to swallow my pride and start over.

When I do anything, I do it big and that wouldn't change because I didn't have anything at that moment. I confessed the successful birthing of my new business, Success & Beyond Global Enterprises, and that it would yield substantial returns so that I would have enough money to travel around the world at my leisure, purchase a new home (larger than the one that I had lost), brand new furniture that I would pay cash for, an extended wardrobe of new high-end clothing to go along with my new lifestyle as a successful entrepreneur, my dream cars including a BMW, Mercedes CLS550 and a Range Rover. Within two years, I had everything that I had envisioned in my mind and declared into the atmosphere while I had nothing at all physically. I was able to purchase real estate property, to bless many others in their time of need by sowing money, food, clothes, jobs and cars into their lives. What a mighty God we serve! Believe and you shall receive! MMM is a way of life for me.

The same rules apply to our speaking-believing, confessing and manifesting our marriage mates into existence. What do you really want in a relationship? Mate? Marriage? Envision in your mind, believe it in your heart, write the vision and speak it into the atmosphere to see it materialized!

WHAT DO YOU REALLY WANT?
If you are serious about attracting your ideal marriage mate, then the manifestation process will require much more that you simply desiring him. You must take more proactive means to realizing your dreams. This is the first step in taking a dream from "dream zone" to realization zone.

Habakkuk 2:2 instructs us to "write our visions and make them plain so that we, and others, will not have trouble seeing, understanding and executing our vision. (emphasis added). It is very important that we understand our vision and are able to move it forward by properly planning to have what we want. Completing this process of writing and planning for the things that we want will increase our chances of bringing those things from dreamland to realityville.

WRITE THE VISION AND MAKE IT PLAIN
We have to set specific boundaries in our lives that are centered on us achieving our goals and not making provisions for our flesh or a contrary way of thinking.

I briefly pointed out a few things earlier that I considered roadblocks to my path achieving personal goals. Some of which were on my Single Wives checklist, and I needed to address my lack of progress in those areas. Although I had overcome many obstacles in business as an entrepreneur and visionary, I could not seem to overcome a few main personal challenges with a major relationship. I had a very troubled relationship with food. My relationship was very addictive in nature, and looking back over the years, the addictive behaviors worked directly against me achieving my weight-loss goals.

In addition, my life was hectic and jam-packed with business and ministry responsibilities-some of which were unnecessary. I was a bit unorganized, scattered and needed to be more timely with scheduling appointments so that I wouldn't miss completing important tasks. The truth is, I would not have been mentally, emotionally or physically capable of adding the responsibilities that come along with marriage, of a husband and children, if I did not make some life changes to prepare. These were barriers to my getting married. I had to make room for my potential mate and free up time to be able to care for my future family's needs.

I began to restructure my life, removing all unnecessary businesses, projects and people to practice a lifestyle of a married person. Maintaining a clean and organized home, cooking, and having sufficient free time for relaxation and other social activities were key in this stage of development to make sure that the things that I desired in life would actually fit into my life. I had to make sure that I was accustomed to working in the role of a wife now so that the shift would not be uncomfortable. After all, I had been living independently for the past three years, and I had to make a mental shift to sharing my life and time with another person in the role of a support.

EXERCISE YOUR MIND, BODY AND SPIRIT

Year after year, I saw in my journals the same old "healthy living goals" that I never fully followed through on and it made me sad. Why was I successful at disciplining myself to reading and studying the Word, praying and working hard to meet business challenges, but I could not seem to succeed at committing to taking care of my temple?

I had to take some real time to address my destructive behavior patterns, to make sure that I was making my health a priority or I would not be able enjoy the successes in business or marriage without being physically capable. I needed to lose weight and exercise more regularly to preserve my temple to the best of my ability.

THE SINGLE WIVES BASIC PRIORITY PLAN: PREPARATION IS KEY

To achieve balance and ensure that all areas of my life were prospering at the same rate, I came up with the following plan that incorporates practicing holistic health habits. The healthy eating tool is located in the Single Wives Workbook, (provided in seminar or workshop sessions) helps you to prepare your mind, body and spirit for marriage. It includes daily regimens of vitamins, supplements and natural and spiritual foods to add to your life. We must have living natural and spiritual food and we must exercise our mind, body and spirit to optimize our performance as single wives.

SPIRITUAL EXERCISE THROUGH PRAYER AND BIBLE STUDY

> » **IN THE MORNING:** Why? This establishes God as a priority and gives Him the very first part of our day before other things begin to take over. We are able to allow ourselves to present our minds and bodies to Him for daily mind cleaning. We will make a habit of dumping out old thoughts and depositing the new thoughts from the mind of God. This daily practice of making God priority will strengthen your relation-

ship with Him and He will give you daily direction, guidance and specific instructions to solve problems. I love me some sleep and it was a huge sacrifice to make myself get up early in the morning to spend time with God. Everyone needs proper rest, and for most adults this can be achieved by sleeping roughly eight hours a day for optimal health results.

» **DURING THE DAY:** Spend a few moments with your vision board, affirmations and biblical promises related to marriage and your other desires. Stir up untapped gifts of creativity. Explore music, art, dance or other creative outlets.

» **BEFORE BED:** Spend a bit of time in prayer, thanksgiving and MMM confessions. You can never confess too much! The more that you say something the more you train your brain to believe what you are saying—the more you begin to identify or actually "feel the emotions" associated with having what you are confessing. And this, my friend, is the major creative force in the entire process-you will create the manifestation through visualizing and "experiencing the manifestation" before it actually manifests into our lives. This is the power of vision and confession—it creates everything that we see in our minds. Try it. I'm a witness that it truly works. I'm looking forward to hearing the testimonies of the mates that will manifest pursuant to you preparing yourself for marriage by applying the insight and wisdom that you have learned within these pages.

MANIFESTING YOUR MATE: SPEAK THOSE THINGS

There are specific steps necessary in manifesting your desires; in this case it is your mate. The first step to successful manifestation is identifying and understanding our "intention" in the matter.

» **STEP 1**

We all must make a conscious decision to seek out what we desire. If you are not sure what it is that you really want, take a moment to imagine yourself living your dream life. If there were not any restrictions on you or perceived barriers preventing you from having your dream life, what would you wish for? A lot of people would wish that they hit the lottery and never have to work again or that they could live a long healthy life with lots of happiness and achieve all of their career goals. The same visions or goals that we set for our education and careers should be set for our relationships. We should have goals and expectations of achieving relational success-attracting our ideal mate, engaging in a loving and fulfilling relationship that leads to a healthy and successful marriage. That is a great basic and attainable relational goal.

To make that plan become a reality, you must see it in your mind, believe in your heart that it can happen for you, and then prepare for it by "acting as if it has already happened" and practicing living the life as if the thing that you desired has presented itself. One way to do this is by daily confessions, declarations or affirmations. By speaking the things that we desire over and over into the atmosphere, we train our brains to believe the things that we are saying and then your actions-will follow. Meaning once you really believe that you are capable of having the type of loving relationship that you desire with your ideal mate, you are more likely to make decisions that are in line with that belief; i.e. disconnecting from dysfunctional relationships, putting yourself in an environment with highly qualified husband material instead of unqualified boyfriends.

Start imaging how you would feel to come home to your mate who greets you with a kiss and has prepared a nice meal for you because you have been working late; feel the embrace of his firm hug and the joy of snuggling on the couch after your meal together. You must take a moment to FEEL the experience of having all of your relationship dreams manifested. Dreams manifested? If you can't picture or feel what its' like, then maybe you are not ready for it, or don't really want it that much after all. Perhaps you may even think that you can't have it or don't deserve it for some reason.

Sometimes we give up wanting something when we believe that we can't have it. Although we don't actually stop wanting it—we just deny ourselves the desire. This is based upon the fear of disappointment, and the fear of disappointment undermines our intentions. We are afraid that we won't get (or achieve) what we want, so we give up wanting, and deny ourselves the opportunity to even try. Feeling 'unworthy' can create this fear. You must want it with your heart, soul and mind then intentionally experience it before it arrives to, actually, manifest it.

» **STEP 2**

The second step in realizing your relationship dreams is commitment to having it. This entails being willing to have it and all that it entails…no "ifs," "buts" or "maybes." Do not be half-hearted or ambivalent about it. You must be precise. This may become difficult when much time has elapsed and the ideal mate has not manifested. You must still be committed to your dream, hold fast to your faith and continue to confess, declare and decree the things that you see in your mind in order to see them in your life. This step requires you to focus upon your true intentions and to experience the commitment and conviction that you have in it. You must be committed to your true desires in order to attain them.

» **STEP 3**

This is all about affirming what it is that we want. Say aloud or write down your affirmations. The more you do it, the better, as each affirmation activates your intention and this begins to establish it in the physical realm. The best example is in Genesis 2 when God created the entire universe by His spoken Words. He manifested everything that He desired or saw in his mind out of absolutely nothing. Just as He created light out of darkness, you will create the reality of your ideal mate out of a period of singleness. Basically, your voice creates a wave-form of energy, and the power of your intention and clarity of your visualization gives the affirmation extra strength and endurance. To visualize the attainment of your mate, you must experience him as fully as you can in the here and now. A "vision board" is another positive way to affirm and manifest your desires. Place pictures on a board of you and your mate, your house, cars, children and other marriage desires such as his attributes, your travel spots and family traditions together. Each of these actions will reinforce your inner conviction and affirms your goals to the Universe.

» **STEP 4**

The fourth step to successful manifestation is to be thankful always in every situation and stage of your life. By being appreciative and grateful for what we already have in our lives today, you create a positive line for more to come into your life. Give thanks for the manifestation as if it has already taken place. Be generous in your thanks and act as though it is already part of your life, and be grateful for it; feel it- own it.

» **STEP 5**

"Let it go" is the fifth step to successful manifestation. Sometimes this step is the most difficult of all as it requires that you release your desire for your mate into the Universe so that your order can be taken, prepared and delivered. You need to "let go" for your mate and other relational desires to come to fruition for you.

Remember to maintain a heart of thankfulness for all that you have, and for all that is yet to enter your life. Use your time in your singleness to sow love into the lives of others. Help friends and family members who may be in crisis and need support. Focus on using your talents, gifts and skills to benefit someone else and that causes you to work in purpose, which positions you for receipt of your desires. Have faith and trust that your mate is on his way to you right now and each day you are getting closer and closer to meeting, courting and enjoying a loving marriage.

» **STEP 6**

Sit back. Relax. Enjoy the adventure of knowing there are great things in store for you and that you are closer than ever to receiving them. You should rest in knowing that you have taken all the steps to successful manifestation of your mate; your prayers have been heard and now you can just wait for miracles to happen in God's divine timing. Follow these steps to successful manifestation of your ideal mate. They can be achieved but belief, confessions/affirmation/declaration or vocal work; patience, faith and trust must be put in on our behalf.

SINGLE WIVES AFFIRMATIONS

Affirmations are a perfect way to "tune yourself in" to the goal of attracting romance and love into your life. This is because affirmations have the power to change your habitual inner dialogue and to set up mental wave patterns that will give you that "good vibe" that you feel when you're around certain people. Have you ever really liked someone and just felt like being around him or her all the time? If so, you'll be relieved to know that using positive affirmations can actually help you to develop that vibe even for your future mate! This feeling, I submit, is actually a major piece of attracting your soul mate into your life.

This is really exciting! Just imagine, you have the power to bring the things that you desire into your life and now you have the strategic tools to begin the process. You are that much closer to attracting your future husband.

You may develop your own affirmations or create variations of the ones below. They are simple and effective love confessions, declarations or affirmations.

FIRST, GET SPECIFIC ABOUT WHO YOU WANT TO ATTRACT

Before you begin writing your love affirmations for attracting your soul mate, you have to get specific about two things:

1. The kind of person you desire or want to attract.

2. The kind of person that you must become in order to attract the type of person that you desire.

Oftentimes, people create positive affirmations about something that they want but never bother to prepare themselves for it or make the necessary changes in themselves that are required in order to obtain and sustain what they want. This is especially important when it comes to your romantic relationships. The first thing you need to do is make a list of specific characteristics that you're looking for in your ideal mate, and then ask yourself this question: What things would I need to change about myself in order to attract this type of person and build a meaningful relationship with them?

The answer to this question is the foundation upon which you're going to build your love affirmations...

BUILD YOUR AFFIRMATIONS

Your positive affirmations for attracting your ideal mate need to have four things in common. They need to be: in the first person; in present tense; focused on the characteristics you're looking for; and most importantly, focused on the characteristics you're going to build in order to attract the love of your life.

For example, if you're looking for someone who is confident and ambitious, your love affirmations might sound like this:

> "As a confident and ambitious woman, I naturally attract confident and ambitious men into my life."
>
> "My confidence and assertiveness attracts confident and assertive men."
>
> "I attract loving and ambitious men because I'm a loving and ambitious woman."

Now, notice that each one of these love affirmations has four things in common:

1. They're all in the present tense.
2. They're all in the first person.
3. They all involve the characteristics you're looking for in a date.
4. They all involve the characteristics you need to attract them.

In case you're thinking that you are being dishonest with yourself in declaring such things, here's something you should note about how affirmations work: Singe Wives Affirmations, like any other affirmation, work to condition your subconscious mind to believe the things that you are consistently telling it. You in essence are training your brain. Once these beliefs become programmed, they'll begin to influence your actions, and beliefs will become a reality. This is because of a psychological principle known as cognitive dissonance.

Cognitive dissonance is the discomfort with which a person feels when their beliefs and their actions are not aligned. This discomfort generally causes a person to change their actions in order to make them consistent with their true beliefs. So as I mentioned earlier, you may not feel like the things that you are saying are true in the beginning but that cannot stop you from doing the work of continuing to confess your desires and affirm your new beliefs about your relational success. You eventually will start to believe everything that you say and then you will align your life to make sure that your actions are helping you to reach your goal of transitioning from Single Wives to Married Wives.

THE LAST STEP IN THIS PROCESS IS TO…
Rehearse Your Affirmations

Once you have written the vision for your future marriage, you must verbally rehearse them in front of the mirror in the morning and in the evening daily. This is where the magic really starts happening…and it will take you a number of days for things to really pick up momentum, but what you'll start to notice is that your creative imagination, your subconscious mind and your beliefs will begin lining up the pieces of your life which are necessary for you to start attracting your ideal mate. How exciting!

CHAPTER 6: SINGLE WIVES MANIFESTO

- » I choose to be at peace with the way that things are.
- » I have faith that my future relationship will be full of love and joy and that it will last.
- » Love is my divine birthright, and I claim it now. I give and receive love fully. I release the past and let love flow into my life now and forever.
- » I am patient with myself and my healing process from the effects of past abuses, hurts and the painful emotions that come along with them. I choose to have the strength to grow forward and be happy.
- » I allow my mind to be at rest with any poor decisions that I have made in my life and am thankful that I have learned from my mistakes. I realize that all things, the good and the bad, are working for my good and have made me a wiser and stronger person.
- » I am open to new possibilities for my future, ones that I cannot even fathom now.
- » I am compassionate with my heart and myself. I have the potential to experience love greater than I have ever known.
- » I am so much more than my body. I am spiritually sound, intelligent, loving, giving and a capable Wife.

- I am willing to let go of people and things that do not support my goals or positively contribute to my life.
- I trust because I am operating in purpose, that life is leading me to someplace wonderful.
- I commit to implement the things that I have learned in Single Wives.
- I push thru. I choose perseverance. I accomplish what I set out to which is attracting my god-ordained mate and enjoying a lifetime of marital bliss.
- This year and the years to come will be wonderfully epic!
- I accept my family for who they are and thank them for the gifts they have given me.
- I choose to see the abundant amount of joy in my life and I am thankful for everything just the way it is right now.
- I am willing to act out of love all the time.
- I use my singleness wisely; I seek out God's plan for my life, His calling and assignment that I am to fulfill in my lifetime and do it.
- I am open to knowing my true spiritual nature so I seek a deep and intimate relationship with God, my creator.
- I am anxious for nothing but prayerful about all things—I allow my thoughts to come, and go, peacefully knowing that I am on the right path.

» I am willing to do the inner work required to resolve what I perceive as my issues. I know that the solutions lie within myself so I choose to heal myself and be happy.

» All is right with this present moment and the best is yet to come.

» I am willing to let my expectations go. Again. And again. And again so that I may seek out life's adventures.

» I have much strength and am an asset to an ideal mate; I appreciate the positive qualities I have received from my family and I let the rest go.

» I choose to put my full focus on changing the aspects of my life that are hindrances to me attracting my ideal mate and sustaining a healthy and fulfilling marriage.

» I choose to wait for a relationship that is healthy, loving and fully supportive rather than settling for just anybody out of desperation.

» I accept pain as an inevitable part of life so I understand that opening myself up to an intimate relationship—trusting someone—I may be disappointed and potentially hurt. That doesn't stop me from pursuing love.

» I choose to listen before I speak and pray about the purposes for all people that come into my life so that

» I may respond to them appropriately.

- I support and encourage others, as I would want to be supported and encouraged.

- I am willing to be uncomfortable so that I leap to the next level in relationships.

- I take charge of my finances and my money is working for me; I have multiple streams of income so that I will never have to stress about money in my future marriage.

- I take care of my temple by choosing foods that will support my body's nutritional needs; I exercise, pray, study and worship God, and detach myself from negative and dysfunctional relationships to maintain good emotional health. This will assist me in being a more capable woman, wife to my husband, and mother to our children.

- I forgive myself for hurting myself by being involved in negative and dysfunctional relationships. I forgive myself for making poor choices in the past. Now, I choose to make only healthy and wise choices for myself in relationships.

- I take time to appreciate all aspects of my life, even the past.

- I trust those who are deserving of my trust. I set healthy boundaries in all my relationships.

- I express my true beliefs by taking the necessary actions to manifest my beliefs and dreams for my relationship.

- » If something/a relationship in my life isn't working, I will evaluate, seek wise counsel, make adjustments accordingly even if that means letting it go.
- » Today I am excited because I've taken steps towards achieving my relational goals. I am closer today to meeting my ideal mate than I was yesterday.
- » I have the courage to act on my dreams without fully knowing the outcome.
- » I am clearly guided toward my higher purpose and I trust that I am effortlessly provided with everything I need in my singleness and future marriage.
- » I continually put energy toward my dreams and they continually become realties. I am thankful that my mate finds me at the right place, time and I will know exactly who he is with no confusion.
- » Love is entering my life right now, my prosperity is increasing every day, and my intuition is guiding me toward right decisions.
- » I welcome change with open arms. Life's timing is always divine.
- » I live permanently in abundance; my life is full of love, joy, peace, wealth and all the great things that I desire including my ideal mate.
- » Today I will give love to everyone I meet. I will speak with love. I will listen with love. I will make loving decisions. I will let love guide me where it wants to go.

- » I believe in myself and my ability to live my dreams. What I think becomes what I see.

- » My new life starts now. (This is a great affirmation to use when negative thoughts creep in or if you feel tempted to fall back into an old behavior you want to change.)

- » Aside from God, my partner is the love of my life and the center of my universe. He loves me as much as I love him.

- » I deserve love, and I get it in abundance. I have attracted the most loving person in my life and life is now full of joy. I always knew that I would be this happy!

- » I love myself and everybody else and in return everybody loves me. Everywhere I go, I find love. Life is joyous—all of the time even in tough times.

- » My partner and I are a perfect match for each other and the love between us is divine. I enjoy his company and he enjoys mine…I am so fulfilled that I can't even remember what loneliness felt like in my singleness. Thank you, God, for presenting me to my soul mate!

The manifestation results are that Single Wives become Married Wives who have obtained healthy and loving relationships with their God-ordained mates. Send me wedding pictures!

Blessings of peace, health, wealth, and relational prosperity!

Thank You Community Businesses for Hosting Single Wives Book Club Events!

#singlewivesbook
www.singlewivesbook.com

ABOUT THE BOOK

SINGLE WIVES ROCK!

This motivational session is designed to empower, inspire, and propel women from singlehood to successful marriages through the art of preparation.

DESTINY DECISIONS

This session helps participants to realize their divine potential in Christ, tap into their purpose and align themselves with God's plan for their lives.

THE JOURNEY TO WHOLENESS

This session digs deep into the hearts and minds of the participants and takes each person on a journey to become free from emotional bondage which prevents us from having successful or truly healthy relationships.

DISCONNECTING FROM DYSFUNCTIONAL RELATIONSHIPS

This session clearly outlines the difference between healthy and unhealthy relationships and explains the importance of recognizing the signs of all forms of abuse.

He who **FINDS A WIFE** finds a good thing and obtains God's favor - Proverbs 18:22

ATTRACT AN IDEAL MATE BY BECOMING AN IDEAL MATE THROUGH THE ART OF PREPARATION
BOOK YOUR SESSION TODAY!

YOU ARE ROYALTY - DATE LIKE IT!

This session teaches ladies the biblical principles of dating for the purpose of connecting deeply with a compatible person who qualifies as a husband or "suitable" marriage mate.

MARRIAGE 101

This session is great for singles or the married alike as it outlines God's original design of the marriage covenant and provides the role expectations for the husband and wife for effective teamwork in the Kingdom.

MANIFESTING YOUR MATE-SPEAKING YOUR RELATIONSHIP VISION INTO REALITY

Most of us plan for everything in life and leave our relationship success to chance...what a fatal mistake! This session teaches us the importance of creating a vision for our relationships and then manifesting it!

The book and seminar sessions are not only for single women, but the message that we should all make wise choices for ourselves in romantic relationships rings true for both single and married women alike. Simply getting married doesn't make you a wife – Proverbs 18:22 says, "He who finds a wife, finds a good thing and obtains the favor of the Lord"...that would mean that you should be a wife BEFORE the wedding! Preparation is the key. – Latezes Bridges

Thanks to Kim Kimble of WE tv's L.A. Hair for supporting Single Wives book!

#singlewivesbook
www.singlewivesbook.com

- » **To purchase additional copies of Single Wives visit:**
  www.SingleWivesBook.com
- » **Follow her on Twitter:**
  @SingleWives2013
- » **Like us on Facebook:**
  Pages/Single-Wives/532828620073846
- » **Subscribe to her Youtube channel:**
  Search "Latezes Bridges"

**Latezes is a contributing blogger for
Jennings Worldwide Blog Community:**

AnnieJenningsPR.com/jenningswire/author/latezes-bridges/

GET YOURS

WWW.SINGLEWIVESBOOK.COM/SHOP

To book Latezes for a speaking engagement, or to host a Single Wives seminar, workshop or conference, please visit

WWW.SINGLEWIVESBOOK.COM and click on 'Contact Us'.

Or, email us: **SINGLEWIVESBOOK@GMAIL.COM**

For business consulting, non-profit start-up assistance, or book writing, editing, or publishing services, please contact: Success & Beyond Global Enterprises, LLC:

WWW.SUCCESS-BEYOND.NET

Make a difference in the life of a family in crisis or an at-risk youth by sending a tax-deductible contribution to:

BEYOND THE BARRIERS OUTREACH, INC.
P.O. BOX 2142, Douglasville, Georgia 30133

Or donate securely online through Paypal at:

WWW.BTBOUTREACH.ORG [Donate Securely]

www.ingramcontent.com/pod-product-compliance
Lightning Source LLC
Chambersburg PA
CBHW071657090426
42738CB00009B/1566